Financial Intelligence for IT Professionals

FINANCIAL INTELLIGENCE FOR IT PROFESSIONALS

The Story of the Numbers

Dr. Julie Bonner

CRC Press
Taylor & Francis Group
Boca Raton London New York

CRC Press is an imprint of the
Taylor & Francis Group, an **informa** business

First edition published 2022
by CRC Press
6000 Broken Sound Parkway NW, Suite 300, Boca Raton, FL 33487-2742

and by CRC Press
2 Park Square, Milton Park, Abingdon, Oxon, OX14 4RN

© 2022 Taylor & Francis Group, LLC

CRC Press is an imprint of Taylor & Francis Group, LLC

ISBN: 978-0-367-62748-5 (hbk)
ISBN: 978-1-032-15294-3 (pbk)
ISBN: 978-1-003-11061-3 (ebk)

DOI: 10.1201/9781003110613

Typeset in Caslon
by SPi Technologies India Pvt Ltd (Straive)

I dedicate this book to all the accounting students I have taught who never wanted to be an accountant over the years. You have helped me learn how to teach this subject in the best ways for the non-accounting and non–finance-focused professionals.

In addition, I dedicate this book to my family, who find creative ways to allow me to take on projects like this!

Contents

Figures and Tables

Preface

As a student, I have had challenges with certain subjects. I believed the idea that girls have a much more difficult experience trying to learn math. Thank goodness I eventually figured out that while aptitude does matter, the teacher can make an enormous difference in a learning outcome. I have spent over 20 years teaching non-finance and accounting majors to learn how to embrace the world of interpreting financial information.

Eventually, when I became a teacher and then tenured university professor, I had to figure out how to build a curriculum that students could follow to learn this material. Through that experience, I learned two essential things: 1) you have to teach to different learning styles, and 2) digital content helps tremendously!

For example, when you learn certain subjects, you may already be experienced in certain things like leadership, management, human resources, and other business topics. Accounting and finance are usually a foreign world to most students. Students are not aware that they have some thinking and experience connections to this subject; thus, I found it helpful early on to connect the material to their lives. For instance, explaining to a student why they have a debit card at their bank is linked to how accounting logic works. Frankly, most people do not see how the world of finance and accounting is something they encounter daily, and they may not realize the connection.

It is best to supplement your reading of the material with other resources. For example, as you study a concept, you can increase your knowledge by searching for YouTube videos on the subjects. I am not the only subject matter expert, and you gain new perspectives by listening to various sources. Having alternatives to learning can break up the monotony of reading words on a page all the time. Many students have told me that the video content and podcast episodes make it easy to learn when on the go, thus creating more opportunities for the information to sink into the thinking pathways.

In addition to all the learning strategy approaches, none is as important as the underlying book. As I delved into the world of curriculum design, there were no textbooks that addressed the non-financial professional. There were a few on Amazon, and I relied on them at first. As different textbooks publishers met with me over the years, I would reiterate that a textbook for the non-financial manager does not exist in their catalog.

Eventually, Taylor & Francis Group saw my vision for a book written specifically with IT managers and entrepreneurs in mind. A written text would bring together the learning strategy, the tools, and the specific accounting and finance situations these professionals could encounter.

In this book, you will learn about this subject in the methods that I find most beneficial to the non-financial professional. You will engage with the concepts, and you will take action in various ways to learn the materials. But the most important thing of all – practice. It is in the DOING that you learn best. I know because I help non-financial professionals do precisely that in my career!

Acknowledgments

First and foremost, I want to thank Barbara (Johnson) Elmore. As a kid, I never thought I would ever learn math. While the accounting world is not a math challenge, it is a conceptual challenge, and I learned from Barbara that the TEACHER MATTERS when learning technical subjects. Without her, this book would have never happened.

Furthermore, there are scores of students that have participated in courses that I have taught who never wanted to learn anything about the world of accounting and finance. These students often did not see the value of learning this subject matter. However, my mission was to help them embrace the numbers, to help each student know that they could gain an advantage in the world if they allowed me to teach them some new skills. A vast majority of those students accepted the challenge. While I cannot name every single one of you, I am forever indebted to your willingness to step up to the plate! My teaching goal led me to many teaching discoveries to get the information across to students.

A huge thank-you to Daniel Kershaw, the editorial assistant to Taylor & Francis Group. There are so many books out there for accounting and finance professionals. He had the vision to see a much bigger market for the non-financial professional to learn how to leverage the information contained in this book!

Abbreviations

EBITDA	Earnings Before Interest, Taxes, Depreciation, and Amortization
EBIT	Earnings Before Interest and Taxes
GAAP	Generally Accepted Accounting Principles
IFRS	International Financial Reporting Standards
SBA	Small Business Administration
SCORE	Service Corps of Retired Executives
SEC	Securities and Exchange Commission

Definitions

10-k is a financial report that publicly traded companies provide to the Securities and Exchange Commission and therefore are available to the public for analysis.

Accounting is the structure and mechanics that create the financial numbers in a business.

Accounting equation is assets = liabilities plus stockholder equity. This equation represents the three sections of the balance sheet.

Accounts payable is a current liability account on the balance sheet representing the total amount of bills owed by the company to creditors.

Accounts payable turnover ratio is a ratio that can be calculated and tells you how often you are paying off the accounts payable balance within a year (a use of cash).

Accounts receivable is a current asset account on the balance sheet representing the open invoices paid by a company's customers.

Accounts receivable turnover ratio is a ratio that can be calculated and tells you how often the accounts receivable balance turns into cash (a generation of cash).

Accrual basis of accounting is where you will record a transaction for your financial statements even if that transaction has not affected the cash balance in your bank account yet.

Activity ratios are the ratios that track the working capital management performance of the company. Activity ratios include ratios of accounts receivable, accounts payable, and inventory.

Allocation is a methodology that a company uses to split indirect costs by hours, production units, or other cost drivers.

Amortization is how an intangible assets cost is spread out over time.

Approval authority is an internal control that specifically and explicitly states who can purchase what and how much for a company.

Asset access controls is an internal control strategy that ensures that assets that have a value that could cause theft are handled in ways that ensure they are not stolen – including asset tags, inventory counts, and restricting access by locked storage.

Assets are items that have value to a company that can be used to generate cash flow. Assets can include property, buildings, truck or car fleets, machinery, inventory, among many.

Audits are a common practice whereby accountants examine the business standard operating procedures, especially those that impact assets, for adherence to policy as a way of determining if a company is at risk with the management of any of its assets.

Balance sheet is a financial statement that gives you information about a business's assets, liabilities, and equity.

Budgeting is a process by which a company, department, or business section forecasts its revenues and expenses.

Cash basis of accounting is where you will record a transaction for your financial statements only when the transaction has impacted the cash balance in your bank account.

Cash conversion cycle is a metric that combines information regarding accounts receivable, accounts payable, and inventory to examine how well these working capital accounts are turning and generating or using cash in the business.

Cash flow statement is a financial statement that analyzes how cash has been generated and used in the company. This is a reconciliation of the cash balance that exists on the balance sheet.

Common stock are offered to the public for an ownership stake in the company. This is a way that a corporation can generate cash by making new offerings of stock on the stock exchange.

Contractors are individuals you hire that are paid separately from payroll and they may only work for you for a project or a shorter period time. Contractors receive a 1099 a year-end.

Cost driver is an activity that drives costs to go up or down. Example: Hiring new employees is a driver of costs of software subscriptions, salaries, healthcare, etc.

Cost of goods sold represents the costs of manufacturing or assembling the products sold or the costs of the services the company provides to consumers.

Current assets are the assets converted to cash in the time frame of a year or less. These include cash (which is are already in its final form of cash), accounts receivable, and inventory.

Current liabilities are the bills due for a company in a time frame of a year or less. The most common account in current liabilities is the accounts payable balance.

Current ratio is a ratio that examines a company's ability to pay its liabilities in the short term (a year or less).

Cycle counting is a methodology that some companies use to manage inventory count. Rather than counting all inventory once a year, you will divide your inventory into categories looking at the value of the inventory and the turnover rates.

Days sales in inventory is a metric that turns the inventory turnover rate into how many days it takes to turn inventory into cash. This is a metric that then can be used in calculating the cash conversion cycle.

Days payables outstanding is a metric that turns the accounts payable turnover rate into how many days it takes to hold on to cash in the accounts payable balance. This is a metric that then can be used in calculating the cash conversion cycle.

Days sales outstanding is a metric that turns the accounts receivable turnover rate into how many days it takes to turn accounts receivable into cash. This metric that then can be used in calculating the cash conversion cycle.

Debt to equity ratio is a metric that assesses how much financing is going on in the company through debt or equity.

Debt to assets ratio is a metric that assesses how much the total assets of a company are financed through debt.

Deferred revenue represents revenue that cannot yet be recognized on the profit and loss statement.

Depreciation is a method of expensing a tangible asset over its useful life.

Direct costs are those costs that can be traced directly to your product or service.

Discretionary income or loss is a term used by individuals to show the amount of money left over after all bills have been paid. It is a comparable concept to thinking about the net income or loss that a company earns.

Draw is an amount of money that a small business owner may pull out of the business rather than taking a salary from the business.

Earnings Before Interest and Taxes (EBIT) is a number that shows you how well the operations are doing in a business. While interest and taxes occur in a business, those are not operating expenses.

Earnings Before Interest, Taxes, Depreciation and Amortization (EBITDA) is a number that takes out the effect of non-operating expenses of interest and taxes and takes out non-cash expenses of depreciation and amortization.

Employees are people that work for you part-time or full-time and are paid through a payroll system.

Equity is a section listed on the balance sheet. Equity represents the buildup of the company net worth through selling stocks (if the company is publicly traded) and retained earnings (the accumulation of the net profits and losses over time).

Equity to assets ratio is a metric that assesses the company's equity compared to the total assets.

Expenses are on the profit and loss statement.

Finance is the interpretation and strategies of the financial numbers in a business.

Financing activities are represented on the cash flow statement that shows how a company is generating or using cash through debt. These balances can represent loans from banks or bonds issued to investors that must be paid back.

Finished goods inventory represents products that are ready to sell to customers. These products often are produced using raw materials or component parts inventories.

Fiscal year represents the time frame of a year that the company uses to generate financial statements. Not all companies start their fiscal year on January 1.

Fixed Assets (*syn. property, plant, and equipment*): Assets like property, buildings, machinery, fleets of autos, or other assets help a company in its operations. These assets will be owned for more than one year.

Flexible budget is one where you develop several versions of budgets, based on various assumptions about inputs and outputs to determine which version best matches the reality of the actual financial performance.

Free cash flow is the amount of cash on hand that has no "demand" on it and thus the company can use it for any purpose. Think of it as the companies "emergency fund."

Gross margin The gross margin represents the difference between total revenue minus cost of goods sold. The gross margin is the money that is used to cover operating expenses, income taxes, and interest.

Gross profit margin ratio is a metric that show the ratio of gross profit to revenue. This number represents every dollar of revenue that will cover operating expenses, interest, taxes, depreciation, and amortization.

Headcount is the total number of employees you have as well as projected headcount in a budget. This can also include contractors for budget line items that use contractors.

Historical averages is a method to look at averages to establish a budget forecast for a line item.

Horizontal analysis is a methodology of seeing how different accounts on different financial statements changed over time.

Income is the amount of money an individual brings into the household. This is compared to revenue for a corporation to ground concepts in finance for businesses.

Income statement (*syn. profit and loss statement, P&L, statement of operations*). An income statement is a financial statement that businesses use to capture the profitability of the company. This financial statement includes revenue minus expenses equals the net profit or loss.

Indirect costs are the costs we know go to servicing clients or manufacturing products, but it is harder to trace these costs directly to the client or product.

Internal controls are procedures and documentation used by businesses to ensure that the company's assets are protected from theft or other misuse.

Inventory is an account on the balance sheet representing the total value of items that are eventually sold to customers. There are different types of inventory and a company may have replacements parts for machinery that are never sold.

Inventory turnover ratio is a metric that determines how many times in a year the company is turning its inventory balance into cash.

Investing activities represent a section on the cash flow statement that shows how a business generates or uses cash from investing activities. Investing activities can be investments into certificates of deposit or treasuries and this can include the investments that a company makes into long-term assets.

Liabilities is a section on the balance sheet that represents short-term and long-term liabilities. This section will include the balance of bills that are owed to suppliers, and longer-term loans and debts.

Limited Liability Company (LLC) is a legal form of business that protects you, as an individual, from increased exposure of legal liability.

Liquidity ratios are metrics that look at the short-term liquidity of the company. Another way to think about it is how well a company can pays its bills in the short term.

Long term is a period of time that is longer than one year.

Long-term assets are the assets of value that will be on the balance sheet for more than a year. This can include items like machinery, property, equipment and other assets that are considered fixed assets. The most common account is called property, plant, and equipment (i.e., fixed assets).

Long-term liabilities are the liabilities of a company that will be on the balance sheet for more than one year. This can include bonds, loans, and other items.

Master budget represents the organization's overall goals in terms of expectations and forecasting of those goals into monetary terms. The master budget then cascades down through the organization into departmental budgets, capital budgets, sales budgets, etc.

Modeling is the development of forecasting, budgeting, or other financial models. These are often developed in Excel, or they pass through Excel for data transformation to get loaded back into financial software.

Net income or loss (*syn. net profit or loss*): This is a line on the income statement (or profit and loss statement). This is the bottom-line number after all expenses have been deducted from revenue.

Net profit margin ratio is a metric that assesses how much money is left over after all expenses have been deducted from revenue on the profit and loss statement.

Net worth statement is similar in concept to the equity that is built up in a company. Net worth is the term used to apply to a person.

Obsolete inventory is the inventory that no longer has a purpose in production, or maintenance, or has met an expiration date.

Operating activities is a section on the cash flow statement. This section represents the operating activities of the business itself – selling products and services and managing all of the processes for the order to cash cycle and the procurement to payment cycle.

Operating expenses are the expenses that a company incurs that are not directly related to the direct sales of products and services. Another way to identify these expenses are the expenses that occur even if a sale does NOT occur.

Operating income is the amount (operating income or loss) left over after costs of goods sold and operating expenses have been deducted from revenue.

Order to cash cycle is a concept that describes the entire process of customers ordering product, the company delivering those products, and turning the sales into cash.

Period of time is a naming convention that happens on financial statements. For example, a profit and loss statement represents a period of time, which can be a month, a quarter, or a year.

Physical counts are a practice of internal controls to ensure that inventory is valued appropriately and being used appropriately.

Procedures are the documentation of internal controls. All internal control procedures should be documented and available upon request. Auditors (both internal and external) use these to verify if procedures are being following as outlined.

Procurement to payment cycle is how a company purchases products and services and then pays for those products/services.

Profit and loss statement (*syn. income statement*) A profit and loss statement is a financial statement that businesses use to capture the profitability of the company. This financial statement includes revenue minus expenses equals the net profit or loss.

Profitability ratios are metrics that are used to assess the profitability of a company.

Property, plant, and equipment (*syn. fixed assets*): Assets like property, buildings, machinery, fleets of autos, or other assets that help a company in its operations. These assets will be owned for more than one year.

Quick ratio is a metric that assesses how well a company can pay its bills in the short-term. However, this is different from the Current Ratio because it takes out the effect of the inventory balance.

QuickBooks is a software product that is very popular among accountants for small business books and reporting. It is produced by a company called Intuit.

Ratios are metrics that examine various different accounts on the financial statements to assess a company's financial performance.

Raw materials inventory is an inventory of individual parts that will be used to produce a finished good. For example, if you build computers, you would have microprocessors, other boards, screens, and various other raw materials that go into the production of the computer.

Reconciliations is a method by which a company can ensure that its assets are fairly represented on the balance sheet.

Retained earnings is an account in the equity section of the balance sheet where the net profits and losses accumulate over time from the profit and loss statement.

Revenue represents the sales of products and services of the company for the period. (*syn. sales, total sales, net sales*)

Revenue recognition is a technique that companies use to determine when a sale will be represented on the profit and loss statement.

Segregation of duties is an internal control that reduces risk of loss of assets by diving up work among several individuals.

Short-term (current) is a time frame that is under one year.

Sole proprietor is the simplest form a business to create.

Solvency ratios are metrics that assess the long-term performance of a company. You can use these ratios to assess if the company will continue to operate into the foreseeable future.

Static budget is a budget that only has one version based on the best assumptions and modeling available to the company.

System access controls is an internal control that assesses who needs access to what systems and functions within a company.

Trendline analysis is a methodology by which you look at historical performance to establish financial data patterns to help forecast a budget line item.

Variance analysis is the process of comparing a financial plan versus the actual financial performance.

Work in process inventory is an inventory that is between raw materials and finished goods. In other words, a computer may be in the assembly process and that would be inventory that is a work in process.

Working capital is a word that is the management of the cash, accounts receivable, inventory, and accounts payable balances.

Working capital management helps you assess how well a company turns inventory and accounts receivable into cash and how long you can hold on to cash before paying off the accounts payable balances.

PART ONE
WHY BEING FINANCIALLY SAVVY MATTERS

Most of the time, if you are a non-accounting and non-finance professional, you can get through most days of your life without having to think much about topics that touch the finance and accounting world. However, as you move through your professional and personal life, there will be times when you absolutely should be familiar with accounting and finance terminology.

There is nothing worse than finding yourself in a professional situation where you do NOT take action because you do not understand this world. You get caught with financial repercussions in a role where having a baseline understanding of these concepts would have helped you avoid pain or embarrassment. The book aims to prepare you for financial situations you encounter in your career progression and how to utilize all resources for your learning.

In Part One of this book, you discover the many reasons why you can help yourself achieve more in your career and personal life if you embrace learning the world of finance and accounting. Of course, you are not training to be an accountant. Instead, you gain confidence in interpreting accounting and finance information that you could encounter in your life, professionally and personally.

Additionally, you work on various situations that prepare you for what would require you to understand the financial impacts of the decisions and choices you can encounter through your professional and personal life. For instance, you will have professional choices, such as taking on a job that requires a certain amount of financial savvy, or you will have personal decisions about investing your hard-earned money. Either way, you want to be prepared for those moments!

DOI: 10.1201/9781003110613-1

Included in this landscape, you will also be thinking about when it might be a good time to move on from an employment situation. People have been surprised with a business closing, and few employees saw it coming. You do not want that to be you! For instance, during the financial crisis in 2009, General Motors went into bankruptcy proceedings. Was it possible to see this coming? Yes, there were clues, especially in the cash flow statement.

Finally, this initial introduction will give you an idea of how you can learn this material. Learning this material is NOT hard, but it does require practice. Thus, you learn the background of why this topic is important and how the book presents your learning opportunity, but you follow a road map on how you can train yourself in learning these topics.

As you start on the topics in this introductory section, some of the information resonates with you more than others. When you are learning accounting topics in other areas of the book, if you are triggered emotionally by understanding the material because of match anxiety or other challenges – come back to this section as often as possible. Figure out which myth or trap about learning this material is tripping you up and re-set your determination. Many students have learned this material and gain a lot of confidence, and I am sure you can add your name to the list!

Topic 1: How Financial Clarity Gives You Professional Leverage

Why would anyone other than a geeky, numbers-oriented, pocket protector-wearing individual want to know anything about the world of accounting and finance? You might be thinking, "I can have a perfectly nice career not knowing anything about this topic." Why should you be open to this information that can bring tangible results to your life and career? Here are a few very tangible reasons to learn about this topic, no matter what your training or background may be in the world of finance and accounting.

Since learning is an activity that requires an investment of time, anyone learning a subject must identify reasons **why** you want to invest in a topic of study, especially since accounting and finance are topics that, on the surface, feel too difficult to comprehend. As you read these reasons, your job is to assess how much these ideas align with your circumstances. Any learning inquiry must have a significant "why," or you will not follow through with learning.

Do You Know If Your Employer Could Be in Trouble Financially?

In 2001, Enron Corporation went bankrupt[1]. In the process, employees lost their retirement funds. Could this happen to you? Is it inevitable that we are at the mercy of others and their financial decisions? Was it possible for Enron employees to question what was going on and have had the insight to see the financial consequences beforehand? Employees can study company financials and see these troubling signs in the financial performance of a company. You have to learn from financial debacles like Enron and other companies to know what the warning signs are to make your own decisions about staying or leaving.

Along the way, when a company is setting itself up for failure, there can be signs of financial distress. The bankruptcy of Enron took a while to arrive. Plus, some decisions do not look like an issue on the surface. In some cases, you may not know exactly how a financial decision is executed. However, the more you study companies you work for and their financial decisions, you will start to see patterns that can cause you to pause and reflect. While you may not know all of the details, you can train your brain and your gut to sense when something might be going wrong, and then you can make your own choices that are best for you, your family, and your career.

Part of your understanding of what to look for will come with a consistent analysis of a company. There are things to think about all along the way. One thing that will help you find these issues is the book sections that show you how to do ratio analysis. However, as you study a company over time, you will become very familiar with their performance, and that is crucial to noticing something going askew in the financial decisions the company is making.

Do You Want to Start Your Own Business?

Starting a business may be your goal. Starting a business may require a significant investment of energy from a person in time and other resources. Small businesses often fail because of fiscal management challenges, especially in terms of cash flow management. Thus, learning about the financial aspects of planning and running a business is crucial to your success. In starting your own business, you will want to know some specific things about finance, such as planning finances, assessing financial statements, and the essentials of cash flow management. People have started businesses with varying levels of financial understanding. Still, those who are successful over time have to understand finances even if they do not keep the books and do the accounting.

In starting your own business, you may want to purchase an existing business. One of the reasons you may want to do that is because you do not want to go through the start-up pains. However, you will want to know how to read financial statements and specific questions you want to ask about the business's financial model in purchasing a business. In this book, you will learn how to do these critical pieces of analysis, OR at the very least, you will feel comfortable hiring a professional to help you!

Do You Want to Grow Your Business or Otherwise Invest in Other Businesses?

For some individuals, you want to study financial information regarding companies that you can invest in with the stock market. Examining financial information is a fundamental analysis that can help inform you about your investment decisions. For most people, these decisions are made by fund managers, and then you can buy into a fund of different stocks. But someone is doing this analysis, and you can learn how to do this analysis if you want to make your own decisions about investing directly in companies.

In addition to investing through stocks, you may own a business someday and decide that you want to grow your business. One way you can develop a business is to purchase another company like yours or invest in a complementary business. When you merge with or acquire another business, you will need to assess financial information and dig into the financial backbone of the company. Either way, you will use the same approach for financial analysis.

The ratio analysis we conduct in the book will give you insight into any company for investment purposes. At first, doing ratio analysis may feel tedious because you have to build your template, and training your mind to understand the numbers can feel daunting at first. However, the book teaches you how to think about these numbers, what they represent, and what they tell you about financial performance. The key to understanding is practice, which is why I suggest practicing on a company your work for or have worked for so that you have the context for these numbers, and that will build your confidence as you start to look at another company.

Do You Desire to Obtain a Managerial, Directorial, or Executive Position?

Some individuals enjoy being in a contributor role in a company. However, for some, the goals are higher. Some people want to move up into management or become a department director or an executive. Regardless of the level of employment, you can impress an interviewer by having some knowledge of the financial aspects of a company. This strategy can be as simple as having read information about a product or service that has been having challenges, and you can ask them about the gross margins on the product. Or that you have seen particular financial performance in the headlines, and you can ask an intelligent question about that to a potential employer.

Topic 2: How Understanding the Numbers Gives You an Edge

It is possible to have great careers and escape having to engage with numbers, but there is a high likelihood that as you advance, or if you want to start your own company, numbers will become a part of your life. It is possible to have an excellent accounting resource, such as an accountant, to work with, but to empower yourself is the purpose of this book. You may still want to employ an accountant, but you will be much more in control if you understand what to look for and how to monitor an accountant. No matter your career trajectory, having a baseline of financial literacy is essential to your career path.

The Difference between Finance and Accounting

Accounting is a specific discipline that encompasses all of the building blocks of how financial information is created. In this book, you will primarily NOT be learning accounting because a large part of the accounting world is about journal entries, preparing reconciliations, and preparing financial statements. Generally, accountants will be tasked with those activities. You will learn specific terms associated with the accounting world so you can ask questions or resolve issues, but you will not be learning the rules of debits and credits, for example.

Finance is the world that encompasses how you use financial information to make decisions in a business. These worlds do overlap, but essentially, you will be more focused on the finance side of this world than the accounting side.

For example, a CFO (chief financial officer), if your company has one of those, will be in charge of all of the accounting and finance functions within the company. Thus, all finance and accounting departments will report up to that role. However, the accounting and finance functions will be split among smaller groups.

Accounting departments would be functions like groups that process accounts payable, auditing departments, manage cost accounting, or process accounts receivable. Finance departments may be functions like capital budgeting, mergers and acquisitions departments, or financial reporting.

In a small business, all of these roles, or departments, might be housed in only a few people who wear multiple hats and perform many of these roles rather than separate departments. A small business will possibly contract out for these roles when they need them.

Utilizing Your Financial Resources Effectively

Besides knowing the numbers and what they mean, you also want to consider how you will take advantage and leverage all the financial resources you have at your disposal. For example, do you know where to find financial information on a company? Do you have a relationship with financially literate people?

Part of your work to increase your financial literacy is to learn where financial information is located and how to assess that financial information. Talk to people about this information, and the more you do this, you will find that you will understand a lot more about this world over time. These habits will help you to develop your knowledge and develop a gut feel for the numbers.

Break Down Silos

We live in a world that encourages people to have specialized knowledge. This approach is great for team members in an organization because you want highly specialized people. However, as you move up in an organization, or if you are going to be an entrepreneur, you may still have special skills, but you will have to learn more about other aspects of a business. As an entrepreneur or business executive, you want to develop relationships and leverage your time through other individuals. Whether these individuals work for you or not, if you cultivate these relationships in the right way, nothing can get in your way of achieving what you want to achieve in business. Even as a team contributor, utilize this time to get to know accountants. There will be tips on what kinds of questions to ask throughout the book, just to help you get started.

Understanding Financial Decisions and the Connection to Financial Performance

If you decide to buy pens for your business, do you know where that shows up in a financial statement? How about purchasing a computer? What if you take out a loan at the bank? What if you need a truck or car for your business? Do you know how to handle that transaction and what it means for your income statement, cash flow, or balance sheet?

You may not know right now, but you will by the time you finish the book. When you know how the financial statements work together as a complete financial information package, you will have a wealth of knowledge that will set you apart in your career. You will know how any decision you make will impact the financial statements. That is informational power that will help you make solid decisions regarding spending, saving, or investing your money.

Assess Promotional Opportunities

At some point in your career, you may find that the next level of promotion will require you to understand some financial information. This knowledge gap could be the concept of budgeting, and it could be expense management, or a capital budget, to name a few possibilities. Does that intimidate you? Does it strike fear in your heart?

With this book, you will be able to understand more about how to manage these tasks. You will be able to establish a framework by which you can understand the mechanics and utilize your resources to address these matters with confidence. Plus, if you are potentially responsible for a department or division, asking for financial information to prepare for an interview is a solid strategy. Then you can prepare questions that will show that you can assess financial performance. There would be nothing worse than taking on a role that no one told you of the financial challenges the group was having, so you want to be prepared to take on roles with a complete understanding of the financial landscape.

In addition, even if a particular role does not ask you to know about these financial topics, you can include questions about products, services, and management of the company by showing that you do understand these topics. The interviewer may not know the answer to your question BUT asking the question will be impressive.

Topic 3: Why Numbers and Accounting Can Be Confusing

You may have tried to learn accounting and finance in the past. Accounting and finance are typically NOT intuitive to learn. Students in accounting and finance classes may have convinced themselves that certain truths exist for not understanding this field of study. However, often these reasons are MYTHS. Part of the job of this book is to debunk these myths and provide you with a roadmap of how you learn this subject.

Myth #1: "I Cannot Learn This Subject Because It Is Math-Based"

While accounting and finance have math involved, you are never expected to do anything beyond simple math. For example, you will need to add subtraction, multiplication, or division in this subject area. You may need to do percentages. However, that is about as complicated as it gets.

The true challenge that accounting and finance present to someone trying to learn this subject is that you must understand the conceptual framework of accounting and finance to make sense of the math. One of the hardest things to learn is the reason for debits and credits; however, we will not dive into that within this book because those rules of debits and credits are most important to a person who creates journal entries. In this book, the audience is intended to be someone that needs to USE and INTERPRET financial information AFTER all the journal entries have been completed. Therefore, as you go through this book, any accounting or finance concept will be explained in a way that connects you to a concrete understanding of the concept. Then the math will be fully explained so that you will know the conceptual framework and the specific application to practice with confidence.

Myth #2: "I Cannot Learn This Subject Because I Am Not Smart"

There can be several reasons why a student may feel this way. One reason might be that the student has never been successful in more "technical" courses. Another reason might be that a student has not done well academically. The bottom line is the teacher can often matter a great deal in how a student learns a subject. My professional teaching life has been devoted to finding the best ways for students to learn this material. My passion for this subject and my dedicated energy to helping students learn have made me successful at teaching this subject. The only students I cannot help are those that refuse to learn the material, and there have only been a handful of students like that in my professional career.

Everything we touch has financial implications to our lives – including being employed by a company or starting your own business. Thus, learning this topic can give you an edge in your personal and professional life. To get there, you must have the following ingredients: a willing student (you), an engaging teacher (me), and the time to practice. Each of these ingredients is equally important. It is rare to learn this field in one lesson or one class, but if you practice, over time, you will gain a solid understanding of the field and what matters to you, and you may very well be surprised at how much you know. I am willing to bet that if you engage with this material, you may be listening to the news or the radio and hear financial information presented, and you WILL realize just how knowledgeable you are in this world of accounting and finance!

Myth #3: "I Cannot Learn This Subject Because It Is BORING!"

While it could be true that any subject is boring, sometimes that viewpoint comes from not having the right teacher for you. You may NOT have known that you could not learn the subject because of the instructor.

An example from my background: I thought I could not learn math. I struggled with math in my early education. I remember being in first grade, learning fractions, and the information would not go in my head. From that time on, at times, I would struggle with math classes. I wanted to go to college and knew that I needed higher levels of math even to be considered for college, so I kept subjecting myself to increasing levels of math classes.

Early in high school, I took algebra I and geometry. I barely survived them. I probably passed because of a grading curve applied by the math teacher. **You do not have to know any upper-level math to learn finance and accounting!** I am only giving you an example to show WHY the <u>teacher matters in learning certain subjects</u>.

In algebra I and geometry, I had a teacher that could get off topic easily. It became a game for my class to ask him questions about politics to divert him from his lecture on the subject material. This strategy was often successful. Thus, I was often left to try and teach myself this subject matter. That is NEVER a good learning environment.

When I came into my final years of high school and took algebra II and trigonometry from a DIFFERENT teacher, I found out why. This woman showed me why a teacher matters in teaching certain subjects. She not only loved her subject, but she also knew how to reach ME. That is extremely important. She knew how students could struggle, and she would frame information in a way that could reach my brain.

The bottom line is this: I find accounting and finance fascinating. I want to pass that love for this subject over to you so that you KNOW, without a shadow of a doubt, that you CAN learn and apply this subject. You do not have to know everything about it to be effective, but if you know that you have a solid foundation to build upon, then there is no stopping you from your professional or personal growth.

The Truth of Why Accounting and Finance Can Be Challenging to Learn

First, accounting and finance is a conceptual framework. Have you ever learned card games or board games? Is it possible to learn how to play chess using the rules of checkers? It would be impossible to learn chess by using the rules of checkers. We know that intuitively. The same is true for accounting and finance. If we try to learn accounting and finance by the rules of math, we are already setting ourselves up for failure. Some of the rules of accounting and finance run counter to any math rules.

Second, accounting and finance, while there are guidelines around the discipline, they are just guidelines. The rules of finance and accounting sometimes are not governed by law – and even if there is a law, as you know, the "interpretation" of the law can matter. Many students want accounting and finance to be clear in the "right" or "wrong" application of the information, and you will often not find that to be true in this world. Just as we hope the discipline of law to have clear "right" and "wrong," you hear many times of cases being thrown out of court on technicalities or someone winning based on the interpretation of a single word. The same is true in the accounting and finance field. There can be laws that govern this field, and there are guidelines, and thus, it can be infuriating to a student that sometimes there is no clear answer. Accounting and finance tend to be taught based on "right" and "wrong" answers, but the truth is, financial performance is a continuum. The more you can accept that, the better you will be able to engage with this information.

Finally, in this world of finance and accounting, there is a lack of standard terminology. Several times in this book, there will be an alert about how various accounts are named or Google information in this book and find different methodologies of doing the same thing. This challenge is probably the single most infuriating thing for a student. However, the book will point these traps out to you to avoid these pitfalls in your learning.

Bottom Line

At the end of it all, know this: I have worked with hundreds, possibly even thousands, of students and clients from many backgrounds and educational levels. If you want to learn this subject, I want to teach it, and that combination will make a successful learning environment for you.

Topic 4: How the Book Is Arranged for Your Learning Journey

It is important to understand the types of activities you can engage with in the book and the format of how the information will be presented for your learning. This section will learn about the different strategies employed in the book to help you apply and learn. It is important to know that application is where the learning occurs – it is in the DOING that you know you can APPLY the information. Think of it this way, simply reading about this subject may advance your skills, but applying the skills will help you know that you can USE the information successfully.

Regarding Readers in Different Countries

This book centers on experience and the rules of accounting in the United States. However, there are two major approaches to accounting guidance and rules in the world – the Generally Accepted Accounting Principles (GAAP) approach and the International Financial Reporting Standards (IFRS)[2].

The purpose of this book is not to teach the differences in rules between the two approaches. The purpose of this book is to teach you how to THINK about what you will find in financial statements. For example, regardless of country, the first item on a profit and loss statement of a for-profit business will be the sales or revenue of the company. In that sense, the information will be the same. However, under IFRS versus GAAP, the treatment or guidance on revenue recognition may be different.

This book aims to teach you what revenue is, what revenue recognition is (among other topics), and to have you feel comfortable reading financial information contained in financial reporting. As you dig deeper, it is expected that you will always have questions, but one book will not cover everything you could need to know. However, this book will teach you where to find information and identify resources of groups and individuals you can contact as your knowledge of financial intelligence deepens.

Relating Personal Finance to Corporate Finance

One excellent way to start learning about the world of finance is to find a place in your own experience to connect the learning to make sense of this framework. The best way to do this is to connect the world of company financial information to your personal financial information. Now, some of you who read this book may never have learned about your financial situation. However, throughout the book and the examples, one method to help you learn will be to relate what you are learning to your financial situation. This may require you to do a bit of extra work to determine your own personal financial situation for some of you. At the same time, this is not a required element of the learning journey.

For example, we may have a budget for each of us, individually or as a family. Maybe we keep track of all money coming into our household and all money going out of the household. Thus, our budget will look something like this (we will go into much more detail later in the book) (Figure 1):

```
+ Income
- Expenses
= Discretionary Income
```

Figure 1   Example Personal Income Statement

For a company, their profit and loss statement will look similar (Figure 2):

```
+ Revenue
- Expenses
= Net Income
```

Figure 2   Example Company Income Statement

For us, as a household, we plan on hopefully having some discretionary income left over at the end of the month, just as a company is looking to have some net income left over at the end of a month. Now, this is rudimentary, just to show you that the process is similar. There are many nuances to learn here, but the mechanism, or the framework, is almost the same. Thus, if you have a budget or know your financial picture, you can use methods in this book to assess your finances, which is a great learning anchor.

Consider the balance sheet and a household (we will go into much more detail later about the specifics of this financial statement). An individual or home has (Figure 3):

```
+ Assets (The things of value that we own)
- Liabilities (The obligations we owe)
= Net Worth (Assets = Liabilities + Net Worth)
```

Figure 3   Example Personal Balance Sheet

For a company, the same approach holds true, with slightly different naming conventions:

A company has (Figure 4):

```
+ Assets (The things of value the company owns)
- Liabilities (The obligations the company owes)
= Equity (Assets = Liabilities + Equity)
```

Figure 4   Example Company Balance Sheet

What to Watch Out For

Periodically, you will see notes about "what to watch out for." This strategy is related to the fact that terminology can be such a problem in learning this subject. Thus, there are words and terms used in the book that can be called different things. Non-standard terms are confusing to students in the beginning. Once you learn the alternative names, it will be easy from that point forward not to be confused by different terms that mean the same thing.

For example, above, in the examples of the income statement and the balance sheet, the mechanism is the SAME. Still, the wording is slightly different between a household financial situation and a business situation. Thus, knowing that discretionary income for a household is the same idea as net income for a business. For a balance sheet, the net worth for a household is the same idea as the equity built up in a business.

Examples

As each term or topic is discussed, you will be given resources to understand everything. This approach includes relating the information to personal examples, but you will also be studying an information technology business. The examples will include a company that is traded on one of the major stock exchanges and a small business examples.

Context

As you learn each topic, term, or calculation, you will be reminded of the context of why you are learning. Either as an employee, an investor, or as an entrepreneur, most of the time, the reasons to learn the topics are the same, and sometimes there are slight differences in how one person may view information versus another person.

Remember, most books and textbooks are written for the accounting and accountant community. Thus, even in college preparations, the average manager does not learn much about accounting and finance relevant to their job. This book is focused entirely on how you can decipher financial information and be aware of how you may interact with this information in your career aspirations.

Exercises

Not only will you have examples shown to you in the book, but you will also have opportunities to practice on your own. It is recommended that you practice as much as you can and get into a pattern of practice. The book will give you guidelines on how this can be done and how your practice can become part of your life to not feel like a heavy burden. By consistently studying this information, you will find that news about companies and their financial performance will take on a new meaning and have much more clarity for you. That, alone, will grow your confidence more than anything.

How to Learn

Throughout the book, there will be pointers and viewpoints about how to learn this material. These are models that give you a way of understanding the learning journey that you are going through, which can be very helpful in understanding the entirety of the learning process and this material.

Remember, some subjects are a little more relatable to our lives. For instance, if you learn about leadership, we often have experience of good and bad leaders. Thus, when we read information about leadership theories and leadership strategies, we have a place for information to hook onto in our brains. However, with accounting and finance, we may have learned a little bit through our personal lives, but there are not many "hooks" in our mind for this information to flow to, so we have to build the learning channels along the way.

Ultimately, the BEST way to learn this material is to read or watch a video about a topic, watch a video or read material on exactly how to think about a process and any calculations that go along with the topic, and then practice it yourself. Not just practice it once, but MULTIPLE times. You want to build a habit, over time, of working with this information, and after a while, you will have built your intuition that right now has very little support structure. By the time you are done with the book and a few months of practice, you will have honed a skill that will divide you significantly from your competition.

Tools for Your Learning

There will be resources throughout the book for you to use. For example, you will be guided to use the 10-k of technology companies. For United States companies that are publicly traded on the stock market, an annual report (the 10-k) must be published to the Securities and Exchange Commission (SEC)[3]. This 10-k has beneficial information that an investor, employee, or entrepreneur can use for analysis. For purposes of examples, the book will compare two technology companies that are currently publicly traded in the United States, Zoom Communications (stock symbol ZM) and LogMeIn (stock symbol LOGM). By studying these two companies, you will see how the numbers tell the story of financial decisions these companies have made over time.

For Zoom Communications, their reporting to the SEC occurs on January 31 each year, and LogMeIn, their reporting to the SEC, occurs on December 31 of each year. Therefore, for example, in this book, the year 2020 for Zoom is the year February 1, 2019, until January 31, 2020; thus, that is the year 2019 since most of the months fall in 2019. For LogMeIn, the year 2019 represents January 1, 2019, until December 31, 2019. Thus, the year 2020 for Zoom Communications and the year 2019 for LogMeIn are the same years for comparison purposes. When you are examining company 10-k forms, you will want to keep this in mind.

For all the examples in this book where Zoom Communications are compared to LogMeIn, Year 1 (YR1) will represent 2019 for LogMeIn and 2020 for Zoom Communications. Year 2 (YR2) will mean 2018 for LogMeIn and 2019 for Zoom Communications.

In addition, it is essential to note that financial statements for LogMeIn and Zoom Communications are in "thousands." This means that if you see a number in this book that is $100,000 (or any number), the TRUE number will be $1,000,000. When you examine the financial statements for these two companies, the financial statements will say (right underneath the name of the financial statement if you are looking at the 10-k document) the numbers are represented "in thousands." Hence, you have to add three zeroes to each number if you want the actual number.

Furthermore, you will be given activities where you can go try out your application of what you are learning in the book. Remember, the first time you go through an exercise, it might take a little bit to get the hang of the process, but if you do these exercises regularly, you will become very efficient in the calculations!

Finally, there are video resources I will point you to that will help with the information contained throughout the book. A video can be an effective way to obtain information. Everyone has different learning styles and having video, reading, and practical exercises will hopefully find the right combination of learning for you.

Other Resources

There is nothing better to teach you concepts than studying your employer. If you are examining your own companies' financial statements, find an accountant who can explain things to you about the financial statements. Now, do not meet with them cold. Do your homework first so that you can take well-informed questions to them. Thus, as you are working on your analysis, you can talk to them about the results or if you have read the financial statements correctly. This approach also gives you the advantage of learning how to interact with accounting and financial professionals. You will want to talk to the person, or group, that produces the financial statements. In larger companies, that will often be a group of people responsible for financial reporting.

In addition to these resources, if you are considering starting a business, the Small Business Administration (SBA) has a group of retired executives that help provide support for individuals planning to start a business[4]. Often, you can be paired with someone with experience in the industry or area of what you want to build, and they are a free resource.

Finally, the company Intuit, which produces the accounting software of QuickBooks, has accounting and bookkeeping pro advisors. However, many of them do require payment, so I only offer that as a possibility the closer you get to implementing a business of your own. If you do start a business, you want to find an accountant that can be a reliable resource in helping you build your business and possibly has expertise in your industry assisting other clients in liking you.

Departmental Learning Groups or Study Groups

If you are in a department where you want to teach your staff financial literacy, you could start a book study group using this book to learn together. The book is written with practical exercises to help you understand the material. Using the book as a framework of studying as a group can make for a rich and rewarding learning experience for the entire group. Thus, as you go along and learn about the different financial resources, you can learn to leverage all the company's internal knowledge to develop financial savvy in each other. By using this approach, you could potentially study a competitor if they are publicly traded.

IF you decide to use this book as a development tool in your department, you recommend that you pull in an accountant in your organization to assist you in the learning. An accountant in your organization will answer many questions for you, like this book related to your products, services, costs, etc. Suppose an accountant in your company is not willing to do so. In that case, any accountant that is comfortable in helping to teach you, i.e., a faculty at a local university or an accounting professional, can help direct you to specific questions to ask your accounting department!

Part One: Exercises, Practice, and Resources

Take some time to think about these questions before you proceed:
- What are your goals for your career as an IT professional? Do you plan on climbing the ladder to a role that requires you to be comfortable with finance and accounting?
- Are you thinking about starting your own IT-based business?
- Do you want to understand more about finance for investing?
- What have been your challenges in the past in learning material concentrated around finance and accounting?
- Which myths about learning this material have you aligned with in the past?
- Do you have an IT-based company that you would like to study along with the material in this book? The company you already work for is a great candidate to study using the concepts in this book! If you do (and it is highly recommended), make sure that you know the stock ticker symbol or obtain financial reports for the company through the accounting department. If the stock is traded on a stock exchange, then you can Google a phrase like "what is the stock ticker symbol for XYZ company." Once you have that ticker or know where you can obtain the financial statements if the company is not publicly traded, then you are ready to go!

Notes

1 Thomas, W. C. (2002). The Rise and Fall of Enron: When a company looks too good to be true, it usually is. *Journal of Accountancy*. Retrieved from https://www.journalofaccountancy.com/issues/2002/apr/therise-andfallofenron.html

2 Majaski, C. (2019). IFRS vs. U.S. GAAP: What's the Difference? Retrieved from https://www.investopedia.com/ask/answers/09/ifrs-gaap.asp

3 Form 10-k. Retrieved from https://www.investor.gov/introduction-investing/investing-basics/glossary/form-10-k

4 Small Business Administration. Retrieved from https://www.sba.gov/

PART TWO
REVENUE AND EXPENSE
The Basics of Income Statements

Before we go too much further, a definition of accounting and a definition of finance would be helpful. For purposes of this book, **finance** is about the interpretation and strategies of the financial numbers in a business, and **accounting** is the structure and mechanics that create those financial numbers in a company.

For example, in creating a financial statement, many details go into that summarized statement. For instance, a company will generate sales, but the financial statement will show only one number for ALL sales. Thus, all that detailed work to create the consolidated sales number is what accounting is all about. However, once you know the total sales for your company and you start analyzing that information, you are getting into the interpretation of the financial information. Thus you are then in the world of finance.

The **income statement** is an essential financial statement to understand[1]. Within this topic area, you will learn why the income statement represents an ESTIMATE of profit. Thus, it is essential to note that estimated profits do NOT equate to the company's cash. There are many reasons for this, and you may find the book repeating information about this critical distinction. The repetition matters – because it is a crucial difference that must be understood to make sense of financial information.

Every section of the income statement will be reviewed to understand the business activity that each section represents. Along the way, you will be given details about different naming conventions, not only for this financial statement itself but for the different accounts represented on the financial statement itself. As stated before, the various approaches to naming conventions will often trip up a student in learning how to interpret financial information. Once you know that one naming convention you see is the same as another different name, then you are far ahead on the learning curve.

In addition, you will be introduced to reporting periods and various other types of information that can be applied to other financial statements. It is good to learn about those topics on the first financial statement you know about so that you are familiar with the issues when they are brought up again on the other financial statements.

Finally, you will also be introduced to the concepts of "cash" accounting and "accrual" accounting. At a baseline level, the important distinction is that cash accounting is like how we manage our checkbooks and bank balance. We, as individuals, operate our lives on a cash basis of accounting. We see money come into our bank account, and we see money go out of the bank account.

However, a publicly traded company must follow the accrual accounting rules. All that means is that a company MUST record transactions, EVEN if these transactions do NOT affect the bank balance yet. Thus, publicly traded companies have a much fuller representation of their financial position in financial statements. But that does mean that you must understand the timing issues that this can mean for interpreting cash flow in a business.

Translating This Information

As you are reading this section, remember that we have money coming into and out of our personal finances as individuals. Company finances work the same way. Thus, a company will generate **REVENUE** from its distinct types of sales to customers (products, services, subscriptions, or gift cards)[2]. However, a personal household will have **INCOME** from various sources.

At the same time, companies and individuals will have **EXPENSES**[3]. Expenses are the services and products we must pay for to run the business or run the household. Thus, a company can pay **RENT** just like an individual may pay **RENT**.

Eventually, after all the expenses are deducted, a business will have a **NET INCOME** or **LOSS**, and an individual will have a **DISCRETIONARY INCOME** or **LOSS**. Regardless of the naming convention, the concept is the same. For a company, the net income can then be deployed in the organization to be in their cash reserves, or the company can choose to invest in capital projects like building a new manufacturing facility, or the company can pay dividends with the money if they have shareholders. For an individual, we can make similar decisions, such as keeping that money in a savings account, investing it, make an improvement on our home, etc.

The ONLY other nuance here is how a company or an individual may account for these items. Typically, most individuals operate on a **cash basis of accounting**, meaning that our profit and loss are built on transactions that flow through our bank account ONLY[4]. Many small businesses work the same way.

However, publicly traded companies have to account for transactions EVEN IF the transaction has NOT impacted the bank account yet. This approach is called the **ACCRUAL BASIS of accounting**[5]. You will be reminded of this concept often through this part of the book!

Topic 5: Profit and Cash Are NOT the Same

It might be a surprise to think that profit and cash are often not equivalent. This concept is important to understand as an employee, an investor, or an entrepreneur. First, we will go through WHY this occurs. Then we will discuss the different major accounts of the profit and loss statement (you will also see the profit and loss statement called an income statement OR you may see it called the statement of operations). This concept will be revisited several times in the book because of the importance of understanding the difference between these two accounts in the financial statements.

Why Profit and Cash Are Not the Same?

To understand why profit does not equal cash, you will have to understand the difference between the cash basis of accounting and the accrual basis of accounting. You want to think about these two approaches in terms of producing a profit and loss statement.

If we think about your finances, you operate off the cash basis of accounting. For example, if you pay an electricity bill, the impact of that payment is felt as soon as you see the money go out of your checking account. Thus, the cash basis of accounting means that we do not record the transaction unless the transaction impacts the bank account. Therefore, if you created a profit and loss statement for your finances, you would use the transactions in and out of your bank account to create that financial statement.

However, if you were to use an accrual basis of accounting, if you had received that electricity bill but you had not paid it yet, you would still include that bill in the calculation of your profit and loss. This approach is true even if the transaction has not been paid yet or cleared out of your bank account. Therefore, in accrual accounting, there can be time lags between recording a transaction and WHEN that transaction impacts the bank account as the money is coming in or money going out.

Procurement to Payment Cycle

The **procurement to payment cycle** is the planning and contracting of purchases, receipt of those purchases, and the payment of the corresponding invoices cycle that occurs in businesses worldwide[6]. Typically, this process will occur like this (with some differences depending on the industry):

A purchase order is created.
The products/services are received.
Invoice is received from a supplier.
Supplier is paid out of the bank.

Now, consider the following table of those same events, and using the cash basis or accrual basis, you will see which transactions would be used to create financial statements (Table 1):

Table 1 Procurement to Payment Cycle

	CASH BASIS	ACCRUAL BASIS
Purchase Order	No transaction	No transaction
Receipt	No transaction	Liability
Invoice	No transaction	Accounts payable
Payment	Cash	Cash

While BOTH approaches do not record any transaction for the purchase order, the accrual basis of accounting is taking that order through a "life cycle" of different accounts marking the various steps to the process.

Think about what this means if you are looking at a small business that you want to invest in, and the business only follows the cash basis of accounting rules. Would you be able to assess, with accuracy, the outstanding payment obligations of the company? It may prove to be difficult. A lot of small business owners kind of "know," in their heads, what they have purchased and what is outstanding to be paid. The reason accrual accounting exists is so that the business owners and investors can see at any point in time what outstanding payment obligations there are at any point in time.

Even the accrual basis of accounting can leave out open purchase orders that have not been received yet. However, at a company that uses accrual accounting, you should be able to ask for a report of all of the open purchase orders, and that will give you an idea of what is coming on the horizon that has not impacted the financial statements yet. Understanding this timing nuance to read financial statements is crucial to your success in making sense of the financial statements and what obligations are outstanding for a company acquisition.

Order to Cash Cycle

In addition to the procurement to payment cycle, there is also an **order to cash cycle** in businesses. The order to cash cycle is selling products and services, delivering those sales, and the payment of the corresponding customer invoices cycle that occurs in companies worldwide[7]. Typically, this process will occur like this (with some differences depending on the industry):

A company sells a product.
A company delivers the products.
A company sends the invoice to the customer.
The customer pays the invoice.

Now, consider the following table of those same events, and using the cash basis or accrual basis, you will see which transactions would be used to create financial statements (Table 2):

Table 2 Order to Cash Cycle

	CASH BASIS	ACCRUAL BASIS
Sales Order	No transaction	No transaction
Inventory Pick	No transaction	Inventory
Invoice	No transaction	Accounts receivable
Payment	Cash	Cash

This book will not go into the specific examples of journal entries that represent this cycle. However, the most important learning here is that more of the cycle is recorded in the financial statements if you are looking at financial statements that are produced on an accrual basis of the accounting approach.

Topic 6: Overview of Profit and Loss Statement

A profit and loss statement is only an *estimation* of profits and losses. Along with that basic piece of information to understand, you also want to make sure that you understand a few other pieces of information about the presentation of information on this financial statement.

Reporting Periods

You can see some interesting dates and time frames for reporting periods for a profit and loss statement. We will first discuss fiscal years and then discuss periods of time. This information is important for being able to compare different companies. For example, in studying LogMeIn and Zoom, in the comparison of financial data, we recognize that the fiscal years are different. It does not matter that they are different; you need to realize that you could get confused by the dates if you are not aware of these different time frames.

Fiscal Years

A **fiscal year** is a defined financial reporting period for a company[8]. You might assume that every company works off a calendar year as their fiscal year. Some companies do use a calendar year for financial reporting, but many do not.

Why might it be different? Very often, the reason may be lost to time and the company memory of when that decision was made, but generally speaking, retail companies are often the companies that can have different time frames other than the calendar year for financial reporting. For example, Microsoft has a fiscal year of July 1 until the following June 30. Thus, when you look at a profit and loss statement for Microsoft for June 30, 2019, you are looking at a financial reporting period of July 1, 2018, to June 30, 2019. There are six months in the previous year and six months in the current year. Many think that summer is a slower time of year, and if you think about it, many vacations happen in the summer, so why not have your year-end activities completed by the time most people are taking a vacation? It could be a reasonable justification.

Also, you may see some companies that have a retail component ending their fiscal years in September. There could be an inventory reason behind the thinking for this situation. The largest amount of inventory for a retail company could occur in the last quarter of the calendar year. Retail companies are getting ready for Thanksgiving and Christmas sales periods in the United States.

Periods of Time

The **period of time** may represent a month or a period of time in terms of four or five weeks. You will be able to tell what accounting periods are being used by looking at the profit and loss statement itself. Each profit and loss statement will say something to the effect of "....for the period....". This "period" could be a specific month of a specific year, or for a specific quarter, or a specific year.

If a period of time for the profit and loss statement is for a month, you may see something like, "Prepared for the month ending August

31, YYYY". Or, if the profit and loss statement is for the year, it may say something like, "Prepared for the year ending December 31, YYYY".

If a company is following a four-week, four-week, five-week calendar, then the month, quarter, or year ending date will move around a little bit. For example, if a fiscal year ends in September, the year-end date could be September 29, September 30, or October 1.

Be Aware!

Sometimes, unusual or extraordinary items show up on the income statement. These items do not occur regularly and will be identified as extraordinary items. These items can have an unusual or variable impact on financial performance, usually impacting net income the most.

For example, in 2013, Starbucks had to pay out a dispute with Kraft Foods[9]. In all of the years of studying the financial performance of Starbucks, every year, the company had anywhere from $.10 cents to $.13 cents of net profit consistently, but in 2013 the net profit was practically zero.

In calculating the net profit margin, if you took OUT the impact of the payout to Kraft, then net profit was still in range of what I was used to seeing in their financial performance. Thus, relying on financial intelligence, the performance was easily explained, AND if all things had been normal, then performance would have fallen in line with any other year studied. Thus, when you see any unusual items like this, calculate financial ratios (see Part Five) with and without the unusual items to see and assess the impact.

Major Sections of the Profit and Loss Statement

The first financial statement to study is the profit and loss statement, the statement of operations, or you may also hear it called the income statement. A **profit and loss statement** summarizes the revenue and expenses for a specific period of time[10].

Here are the major accounts to understand that appear on this statement:

Revenue

Revenue represents the sales of products and services of the company for the period (this may be a month, a quarter, or a year). When you are examining a profit and loss statement, this account could be called revenue, net revenue, sales, or net sales. When you look at one month of revenue or one quarter, or one year, that may not tell you much about performance. Thus, when you are examining any financial information, you will want to look at trends over time to get an idea of consistent performance over time.

In a profit and loss statement built through the cash basis of accounting, you would know that this represents the cash that has been paid to the company, and the money has already been received at the bank. Suppose the profit and loss statement has been built using the accrual method. In that case, it will be important to understand how much cash is still outstanding as represented by accounts receivable on the balance sheet.

Another important thing to watch for here is the typical treatment and timing of different approaches to recording revenue under the accrual method. You will want to be clear on the timing differences between gift cards, credit card transactions, and invoicing. Here we will consider each one of these and the timing issues each can create.

First, consider a credit card transaction. In this scenario, a customer buys a product from you and pays for it with a credit card. The timing between sending the customer the invoice and getting your cash is short. Depending on the credit card company, the cash will be in your bank account within 24–48 hours. Thus, the timing of converting accounts receivable to cash will look like this (Figure 5):

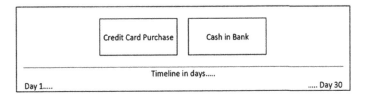

Figure 5 Credit Card Transaction Timeline

Second, if you allow your customer to have 30 days to pay their invoice, you will have to wait for the cash a bit longer. The same mechanisms are in place, i.e., you send an invoice to the customer, but the customer can take several more days to pay. Thus, the accounts receivable will be sitting on the balance sheet for a longer period of days. The timing could then look like this (Figure 6):

Figure 6   Customer Invoice Transaction Timeline

Finally, if you sell gift cards, cash timing works very differently. The most significant difference about cash and revenue timing in these transactions is that the company receives the CASH before the REVENUE is recorded. In other words, a gift card is not a product, and it is a promise of providing a product later. Thus, if a customer obtains a gift card and places $100 on the gift card, the company gets the use of that cash once deposited into the companies bank account. The customer may not take delivery of a product until the following week or several months later, and only when the actual product is obtained, the company keeps that $100 value on the balance sheet as a liability. This process is commonly referred to as **deferred revenue**[11] (Figure 7).

Figure 7   Gift Card Transaction Timeline

Cost of Goods Sold

Cost of goods sold represents the costs of manufacturing or assembling the products that are sold or the costs of the services the company provides to consumers[12]. When you examine a profit and loss statement, the cost of goods sold account is subtracted from the revenue. Sometimes, you will find a profit and loss statement that calls this account cost of revenue.

Cost of goods sold has a timing effect that needs to be understood as well. Plus, this account on the profit and loss statement is estimated and reconciled to actual costs at the end of the year. How does this happen?

For example, if your company builds computers, you will be buying motherboards, screens, keyboards, and other items that go into building a computer throughout the year. For example, suppose that you receive 100 screens this month. Will you build 100 computers this month? Maybe you will, but will you also sell those 100 computers in the same month? Most likely not.

When you think about a company like Lenovo that build computers on a grand scale, when inventory is received when a computer is sold could be more than 30 days.

In addition, think about how you build a computer. For some people, starting a business out of their garage, you might build one computer, by hand, in a few hours. However, building computers on a massive scale will require some investment in equipment to either help automate the process, if you can, or at least make moving computers from station to station more efficient.

Thus, building a computer from scratch and by hand will require you to have parts on hand and a person to do the labor of building that computer. The same is true in a larger company. The only difference is you may build a lot fewer computers because of a lack of automation (Figure 8).

Figure 8 Product Inventory Timeline

Gross Margin

Gross margin, or gross profit, is a straight calculation. Gross margin is the difference between revenue minus cost of goods sold[13].

Gross margin, on the profit and loss statement, is a calculated number. You will take the revenue for the period, subtract the cost of goods sold, and you will arrive at your gross margin. Gross margin represents the difference between what you sell your products and services for and the costs it takes to provide/manufacture those products and services.

Think of it this way: If you sell a product or service, you will have costs directly associated with that sale. Another way to think of this is typical, and if you do not have any sales, you will not have any cost of goods sold.

Operating Expenses

Operating expenses are the expenses that it takes to run the company with no connection to the cost of sales (or the cost of goods sold)[14]. For example, suppose you have a company that manufactures a product. In that case, the product manufacturing costs will be reflected in the cost of goods sold, and the sales of the product will be reflected in revenue. The operating expenses will be the other kinds of costs to run the business – the administrative departments that are NOT part of the manufacturing and delivery of products or services.

Operating expenses are the costs of running the business in general. Another way to think about this is what are the costs that you must pay, in the business, that have nothing to do with selling products or services. For example, office rent for an administrative office is an operating expense. If you ever ask, "what does it cost me to run my business" then the portion of the operating expenses of the income statement is where you would look for the answer.

Thus, within this section, one of the largest accounts will be called something like "Sales and General Administration." You might even hear this called "SG&A." All the expenses for information technology departments, legal departments, sales and marketing departments, accounting departments, and others.

Do not confuse operating expenses with the expenses associated with the manufacturing part's operations. Expenses associated with the operations of the manufacturing and distribution part of a business will be in the cost of goods sold. For example, if you sell computers, there is a cost to building or sourcing a computer that is directly associated with the sale. Also, if you provide information technology consulting services, then one of your highest direct costs of providing those services will be the cost of the labor (consultants).

Another way to think about this is to consider what happened in the COVID-19 pandemic experienced worldwide in early 2020. Many small businesses and large businesses found themselves in a period of time where they may not have made any sales. However, even if they did not make any sale in a particular month, the company would still have operating expenses to pay. This concept is why a company needs to set aside its cash for a rainy day, just like each of us running a household needs to do!

Operating Income

Operating income is the amount left over from gross profit after operating expenses are deducted. It is a straightforward calculation of gross profit minus operating expenses equals operating income[15].

Net Profit

Net profit is the bottom-line number of the amount of money that is left over after all the expenses have been deducted[16]. One of the more common items deducted after operating income are things like interest expense. Interest expense accounts are the number of interest payments for bonds that have been issued. Since bonds are a financing strategy by a company but have nothing to do with running a company, these line items always come after the operating income.

Topic 7: Breaking Down the Profit and Loss Statement

A fundamental concept to understand is the interplay between revenue, cost of goods sold, and gross margin on the profit and loss statement. These are the first three major groupings of items you will see on a profit and loss statement.

What do you want to see in this section? Well, one thing you want to see is that revenue is consistent over time and possibly growing. You want to know that cost of goods sold is consistent, and it might grow in relation to revenue if revenue is going up. However, the key factor here is that the gross margin remains steady and consistent.

What this means is that industries typically have a range of gross margins within industry. For example, restaurants tend to operate on smaller gross margins. However, some higher-end restaurants could work off better margins, and it will depend on your business model. Still, typically speaking, restaurants can go out of business more often in economic downturns because the margins are thinner. Computer technology companies can enjoy significantly higher gross margins because the technology sometimes does not cost a lot to produce.

In addition, another reason this matters a great deal is that when you are starting a business, you want to make SURE that you understand what it COSTS to produce your product or service. For instance, a colleague, who works with companies on marketing and sales strategies was hired by a restaurant and the restaurant wanted her to help them increase sales.

This colleague had the smarts to ask the owners about how they planned out the costs of each meal they prepared. By analyzing this data first, it was discovered that there were mistakes in the recipes of the dining options and some math mistakes. Thus, even if she had brought in more business, the restaurant would have lost even more money. Once the restaurant corrected the pricing issues and had a good, accurate margin, several cash flow problems started to dissipate. Then, working on sales and marketing strategies made sense.

Now, in the case of technology companies, gross margins can usually be excellent. Technology companies usually have nice hefty margins because technology companies can often take advantage of lower production costs. According to Wilhelm (2019), technology-based companies can enjoy gross profits that are usually above 50%[17].

Thus, technology-based companies are usually generating cash with smaller costs of production. Later, in the book, you will be assessing the gross margin and net margin of any company. These financial metrics will tell you just how well a technology company can leverage the most profits that it can by lowering costs. In addition, you will also be examining how well a company manages its cash flow. You will be able to assess this through the cash flow statement itself and the activity, or efficiency ratios, of accounts receivable turnover, inventory turnover, and accounts payable turnover and how all of these ratios inform the cash conversion cycle of a company.

Revenue Recognition and Timing Issues

Here, you will dive into a bit more detail as to why timing issues are at the heart of why profit does not equal cash. We will focus first on revenue recognition and why there are timing issues with cash when examining this concept.

First, **revenue recognition** is the idea that revenue is recognized at a point in time, generally when products or services are exchanged between the seller and the buyer[18]. There are some exceptions to that rule, but this is a general idea.

So how does this play out in reality? Here are two examples:

First example: You are a technology company that sells motherboards for computers. A computer manufacturer orders a shipment of motherboards from you for $100,000. Your company has given the customer 30 days to pay the invoice. The purchase is made on July 10, the shipment goes out on July 15, delivery will be made on July 20, but the invoice is due on August 15.

In this case, you are receiving the cash AFTER the product has been delivered to the customer. Using this example, the day that is important for the profit and loss statement is July 15 – because that is the day that typically "ownership" of the motherboards passes from your company to the customer. That is also the date that the invoice is generated. Thus, on July 15, the profit and loss statement will show a revenue item for $100,000.

However, July 15 is NOT the date that your company will receive the cash from this transaction. Since you have given the customer

30 days to pay, the expectation is that you will have the money come into your bank account right about August 15, when the terms are due. Even though revenue is in the profit and loss statement on July 15, you will have a corresponding accounts receivable item on July 15 because you have NOT received the cash yet. When the cash is received on August 15, then the accounts receivable will be cleared out, and cash will come into the bank account. How quickly the money is actually in the bank will depend on HOW you are paid – if the amount is paid by check, or credit card, or a bank-to-bank transfer will potentially make the process quicker or add a few days to the process.

Second example: Suppose that you are an educator on technical products, and you own an online store that is full of classes that people can take at their leisure once purchased. Most of your courses sell for $50 per enrolled student. You also run promotions around Father's Day, Mother's Day, Christmas, and other holidays, selling gift cards for any amount from $100 to $500. Suppose someone has gone online and purchased a $500 gift card for a Christmas gift for someone to buy courses from your site.

In this situation, you are receiving the money BEFORE any product is exchanged with the customer. The gift card itself, that little piece of plastic, is NOT a product. That gift card represents a liability to your company because you owe whoever receives this card $500 worth of classes. The person who receives the card could purchase the courses next week, next month, next year; you never know when the customer will claim the products. However, you can use the cash from selling that little piece of plastic as soon as the cash is in your bank.

When the piece of plastic is sold (the gift card), your business will receive $500, but that amount will also show on your balance sheet as an owed liability. Until the customer comes forward, with the gift card, to claim the courses, ONLY then will you recognize revenue on your profit and loss statement, and the liability will be removed from the balance sheet.

Therefore, later in the book, you will be learning about ratio analysis. One of the ratios directly related to revenue and cash is the accounts receivable turnover rate and the days' sales outstanding.

Third example: Another revenue recognition pattern is when subscriptions are used or annual billing for service. In these cases, if a person pays for an annual subscription to your service, and the customer pays the one-time payment for the whole year up front, you are not allowed (if you are under accrual accounting rules) to recognize all of that revenue at the time of payment. Instead, your company will have received cash for payment, but you will recognize 1/12th of the annual subscription each month for the term of the service.

If you take the 2019 LogMeIn (LOGM) 10-k pdf file or the Zoom Communications (ZM) 10-k pdf file, and you search for "revenue recognition," you will find a few areas contained in the document that pertains to this rule. For LOGM (2019) 10-k, for revenue recognition, you find that "we derive our revenue primarily from subscription fees for our premium services" (p. 37)[19]. Currently, a yearly subscription for one of LOGM's products is $349.99[20]. Without considering any tax collections that may have to be completed on a purchase, the base price must be spread over 12 months or reporting periods. Thus, if the sale of a subscription is made in July, the company can recognize 1/12 of the total. Thus, in July, the company can realize $29.17 in revenue ($349.99/12), and the company will have 11 more months to recognize the remaining $320.82 of the subscription rate ($349.99 − $29.17). This concept represents the **deferred revenue** that will be recognized over the remaining life of the subscription.

For the 10-k for Zoom (2019), you will find that "we derive revenue from subscription agreements" (p. 46)[21]. Furthermore, according to the 10-k for Zoom (2019), "contract liabilities consist of deferred revenue" (p. 47). With Zoom, customers can buy a product on a monthly subscription or an annual subscription[22].

Therefore, if you buy the Pro subscription every month, Zoom will recognize $14.99 per month in revenue. In this case, there would be no deferred revenue. However, if a person obtained a Pro annual subscription for $149.90, then the first month, Zoom will recognize $12.49 in revenue ($149.99/12). Then the company would have a remaining deferred revenue balance of $137.50 ($149.99 − $12.49) that will be recognized over the next 11 months.

What happens if you are not publicly traded? For instance, you could be evaluating a company to purchase that will start your entrepreneurial career. The same rules do not bind a company that is not publicly traded. For instance, a small business could be operating under the cash basis of accounting; thus, they recognize revenue as soon as the money comes into the bank.

Thus, you could be looking at a company that creates software that consumers subscribe to for $99 for the entire year. As soon as the $99 comes into the bank, the company may recognize the whole amount. The issue is that the entire $99 should be spread over the year because of rules around revenue recognition are important to follow.

If you acquire a company, one thing to think about is how to move the company from a cash basis to an accrual basis of accounting. You never know when a publicly traded company may come to you and want to acquire your business. In preparations for that possibility, as your company matures, you may want to consider moving more toward an accrual basis of accounting methodology, which will mean that the $99 annual subscription would be spread over 12 months. Thus, you would recognize $8.25 in revenue each month. This approach will take a small project to get this changed in your processes and procedures, and you may need some accounting support and your information technology department to make that happen. Being able to show a potential acquisition partner that you are already operating your small business as a corporation could be very attractive to a potential buyer.

Deeper Dive into Cost of Goods Sold

In the book so far, cost of goods sold has been described as the costs that it takes to produce and deliver a product or service directly. Well, what *exactly* does this mean? Especially when it comes to being an entrepreneur, this idea can be very murky. For any of you working in a company, you can ask the accountants about how they identify costs directly related to producing the products or services of your company.

Remember when we discussed the fact that terminology is a large part of the challenge to learning about the world of accounting? Here you see where terms can get confusing as well. For instance, when you look at definitions of cost of goods sold, the description will be that these are the DIRECT costs of producing goods and services. However, within the cost of goods sold, you can have direct and indirect costs. The confusing part is that you see the term *direct* and that it is being used in two slightly different contexts.

Thus, the cost of goods sold is considered a direct cost of producing goods and services because we cannot classify those costs as general operating costs. However, costs of goods sold can comprise direct costs and indirect costs. So, we need to break this down into an example.

If you have a business that builds computers, it is often very clear that direct materials and labor costs produce the computers. For instance, you will have a technician that builds that computer – so if that is all the technician does during the day. All of the salary and benefits for that person goes into the direct costs of building the computer, and this will definitely need to be a part of the costs of goods sold.

Plus, the parts that go into the computer would be direct costs that go into the cost of goods sold.

What are some of the direct costs that could be considered? Here are some of the items you may consider to source for the computers:

- Central processing unit
- Hard drive
- Screen
- External ports
- Memory
- Drives
- Keyboard parts

Of course, you may also want to think about what peripherals you may want to sell, either separately or in a bundle. These types of items you may buy elsewhere and mark them up within a bundle of products. Items to consider are mice, keyboards, external screens, and other items.

However, what about if this computer production was confined to a single building where all computer production was completed? Maybe many technicians are working in the same building, and there is an inventory warehouse that keeps them supplied with computer parts. So, what about the forklift drivers that bring pallets of parts to the technicians? Many would consider the forklift workers to be *indirect* in producing the computers. The forklift workers are not directly building the computers, but they are assisting the process. Very often, if production is enclosed in a building or set of buildings, all those costs of running the facility would be a part of the cost of goods sold as either direct costs of production or indirect costs of production.

Especially for a business that sells products manufactured or assembled, lenders will EXPECT to see that you understand and account for the cost of goods sold. If you search through the 10-k's for the two companies studied in this book, you will find that "cost of revenue" is the account used rather than "cost of goods sold." Now, these two companies have largely moved to digital formats for their software solutions.

Do you remember buying a disc with the software code embedded in it that you would install on computers? That seems to be a bygone era. Today, we install software from executable files that can be housed on the cloud. Thus, if you search through LogMeIn and Zoom 10-k files, you will see that cloud hosting is often a direct cost of developing and delivering digital products.

In addition, you will find that software development costs are amortized over time. For example, in the balance sheet section of this book (Part Three), there is information about assets and depreciating those assets over time. Software development is an asset; the software has value, it can cost millions of dollars to develop software from scratch, and new additions and enhancements to the product can cost a lot of money.

Thus, assume that you have a software idea and it takes $20M to develop the initial version of the software. Just like buying a building, you would not likely take the hit on the income statement for the total cost, and you would instead capitalize the costs and write it off over, say, 20 to 30 years. When you see "amortization," think of it as "depreciation" for a digital asset. For example, Zoom software and LogMeIn software, even as digital products, have an enormous value to both companies, and they cost quite a lot of money to develop. Just like it can take a lot of money to build a tangle asset like a building.

Part Two: What to Watch Out For

- Profit and loss statements are also called income statements, P&L statements, or statements of operations.
- Be aware that financial statements can be reported with three zeros or six zeros left off the numbers. Thus, if a statement says it is reported "in thousands," you will add three zeros to the numbers. Or, if the statement says the numbers are reported "in millions," then the numbers will need six zeros added to them to know the full value of a line item on the financial statement.
- Revenue is synonymous with sales, net sales, or net revenue.
- Cost of goods sold can also be called cost of revenue or cost of sales.
- Remember, profit and cash are often not the same things, especially when a company is not operating off a cash basis of recording transactions.
- Determine if subscriptions drive revenue. Determine if the subscriptions are monthly or annual or a combination of both.
- Many small businesses work on a calendar year as a fiscal year, but publicly traded companies may not work off a calendar year as their fiscal year. Be clear about the fiscal year so that when you are examining documents, you do not get confused with dates (especially if you are comparing companies).
- Many companies also use reporting periods of calendar months. However, not every company uses calendar months. Some publicly traded companies will use a 4-4-5 monthly calendar system so that every reporting period ends on a Friday or Sunday. This can also be important for your assessment of company financial data because dates could be confusing to you if you do not have that framework understood in your mind.

- Deferred revenue is a mechanism used by companies to store revenue that has not been earned yet. Make sure that you understand if the company uses deferred revenue or recognizes revenue on a cash basis.
- Revenue and cost of goods sold are directly related to the sale of products and services.
- Operating expenses are expenses that occur in a business regardless of whether the company has made any sales or not.
- Technology companies are often companies that can have higher gross margins than a lot of other industries. It is important to know what is normal for your industry.
- If you are studying a company you work for, find an accountant to help you. Finding answers on your own is fine, but part of the learning is to leverage the available resources!
- Suppose you are studying a company that you do not work for nor have worked for in the past. In that case, you will have to rely on Internet searches possibly to find answers to questions that you may struggle with, or you can possibly find an accountant in your network that might be willing to assist your learning journey.
- Watch for extraordinary items. If you find something unusual or is not a regular occurrence, be sure to run your analysis with AND without the extraordinary items.

Part Two: Exercises, Practice, and Resources

Learning activities:

1. Conduct a search on "revenue," "revenue recognition" in the 10-k of your selected companies, and what do you learn about the business and how timing issues work in the company?
2. If you work for a company that you are studying, you can book a time with an accountant, take them to coffee, and learn about how the company's timing of cash and profit work. Several different accountants could help explain how this works in your company, and some examples of

accountants to reach out to are: accounts payable managers, accounts receivable managers, and cost accountants.

3. Look to see if you can find deferred revenue on the balance sheet. Search for the 10-k (or other financial notes) to determine if any notes explain deferred revenues for the companies you are studying.

4. Establish if the companies use a subscription model. If they do, ask them how they handle those subscriptions from a revenue recognition standpoint. Or, see if you can find notes on this in the 10-k.

5. Do the companies you are studying have gift cards? How do they handle this, and can you find notes in the 10-k about how much cash is being generated from these activities? How does the company handle balances that appear not ever to be used to exchange for products and services? What rules do they use to write those amounts off of the balance sheet?

6. Can you find any information about why the fiscal year works as it does for the company you are studying? Why might it be different than a calendar year?

7. What questions pop up for you as you research your chosen company? What resources in the company can you tap beyond the 10-k to help answer those questions?

8. Pull at least five years (more if you have access to more years) of income statements. Are the accounts growing? Are expenses growing faster than revenue? Is there steady growth in numbers, or does each year show a lot of variation? Use the principles of horizontal analysis in Topic 20 of this book to prepare the calculations.

9. What types of costs are in the cost of goods sold? How does the company calculate the cost of goods sold?

10. Does the company use standard costs in the cost of goods sold? How are they calculated?

11. How does the company establish mark-ups on products and services? A couple of sources for this might be a purchasing department or the accounting department.

12. What is the gross margin on the consolidated income statement?

13. If you have access to more detailed information on different products or services, calculate the gross margins. Do certain products subsidize other products? Are all products profitable? If you can dive into more granular detail, then you can find some interesting things sometimes. Sometimes, a company may have "loss" leader items that get customers into the store.

14. What all is included in operating expenses for the company? Many different types of expenses go into administrative expenses, so do as much of a deep dive into this account as you can. You may not have access to this type of information unless you work for the company. Otherwise, you may only be able to find what you can discover in the 10-k.

15. Are there any extraordinary or unusual items on any income statement? If there are, look for notes about those on the 10-k – they should be explained.

16. Are revenues, gross margins, and net profits staying consistent over time? What is the trend?

17. Most often, you may be comparing year over year. However, you can also compare quarter to quarter, or first quarter to first quarter, or second quarter to second quarter. Different ways of slicing the data can give you specific insights!

18. At this juncture in your study, which company is performing best?

Notes

1 Income statement – definition, importance, and example. Retrieved from https://www.zoho.com/books/guides/what-is-an-income-statement.html#:~:text=An%20income%20statement%20is%20a,financial%20health%20of%20your%20business.

2 What is revenue? Retrieved from https://corporatefinanceinstitute.com/resources/knowledge/accounting/revenue/

3 What is an expense? Retrieved from https://corporatefinanceinstitute.com/resources/knowledge/accounting/expenses/

4 Cash basis of accounting (2021). Retrieved from https://www.accountingtools.com/articles/what-is-the-cash-basis-of-accounting.html

5 Accrual basis of accounting definition. Retrieved from https://www.accountingcoach.com/terms/A/accrual-basis-of-accounting

6 What is procure to pay? Retrieved from https://www.ariba.com/solutions/business-needs/what-is-procure-to-pay#:~:text=Procure%2Dto%2Dpay%20is%20the,and%20reconciliation%3B%20invoicing%20and%20payment.

7 Step by step: What you should know about the order-to-cash process. Retrieved from https://www.salesforce.com/products/cpq/resources/what-to-know-about-order-to-cash-process/

8 Fiscal year (FY): definition and importance (2021). Retrieved from https://smartasset.com/taxes/fiscal-year

9 Starbucks, (2013). Starbucks Concludes Packaged Coffee Dispute with Kraft. Retrieved from https://stories.starbucks.com/press/2013/starbucks-concludes-packaged-coffee-dispute-with-kraft/

10 Reiff, N. (2020). Profit and Loss Statement (P&L). Retrieved from https://www.investopedia.com/terms/p/plstatement.asp

11 What is deferred revenue? Retrieved from https://www.accountingcoach.com/blog/deferred-revenue#:~:text=Deferred%20revenue%20is%20money%20received,be%20reported%20as%20a%20liability.

12 What is cost of goods sold (COGS) and how to calculate it. Retrieved from https://www.freshbooks.com/hub/accounting/cost-of-goods-sold-cogs

13 What is gross margin? Retrieved from https://www.accountingcoach.com/blog/what-is-gross-margin

14 Examples of operatings expenses (2021). Retrieved from https://www.accountingtools.com/articles/what-are-examples-of-operating-expenses.html

15 What is operating income? Retrieved from https://corporatefinanceinstitute.com/resources/knowledge/accounting/operating-income/

16 What is net profit? Definition and examples. Retrieved from https://marketbusinessnews.com/financial-glossary/net-profit-definition-meaning/

17 Wilhelm, A. (2019). Gross Margins, Revenue Multiples, and 2019 IPO's. Retrieved from https://news.crunchbase.com/news/gross-margins-revenue-multiples-and-2019-ipos/

18 What is revenue recognition? Retrieved from https://corporatefinanceinstitute.com/resources/knowledge/accounting/revenue-recognition/

19 LOGM (2019). 10-k. Retrieved from sec.gov at https://www.sec.gov/ix?doc=/Archives/edgar/data/1420302/000156459020004769/logm-10k_20191231.htm

20 Logmein.com, subscription pricing. Retrieved from https://www.logmein.com/buy

21 Zoom (2019). 10-k. Retrieved from https://investors.zoom.us/sec-filings/sec-filing/10-k/0001585521-20-000095

22 Zoom.us, subscription pricing. Retrieved from https://zoom.us/pricing

PART THREE
ASSETS, LIABILITIES, AND EQUITY
Understanding the Balance Sheet

One of the first things to know about a **balance sheet** is that the statement sections **MUST BALANCE** (hence the name)[1]. You may also hear accountants referring to this as the "accounting equation[2]." They are talking about the balance sheet because the total value of ASSETS must qualify the total value of the **LIABILITIES** and **EQUITY** in the company. The entire structure of how financial statements are built (in software like QuickBooks, SAP, ORACLE, or any other software that generates financial statements) is based on this idea of "balance." However, that is a topic for your accountant to understand, but the balance sheet must balance is what you need to know. Thus, you would know something is severely wrong in the company financials if the balance sheet was out of balance.

Assets will represent different items that have value to the organization and will be used in the business. Liabilities will be the items that a company owes, either short-term bills that are due like having to pay a vendor or long-term amounts owed like a 10-year loan that must be paid back to a creditor. Equity, in a business, is where all your profits in the business go. If you are publicly traded, the common stock will be valued in this section.

Periods of Time

For a balance sheet, the balances in the accounts continue to grow or decline over time, in Topic 6, where we discussed the fact that a profit and loss statement represents only a specific time frame. Thus, a profit and loss statement may be only for the month of August.

DOI: 10.1201/9781003110613-3   **47**

However, a balance sheet is an *accumulation* of all of the transactions made over the company's life. When you look at a balance sheet, instead of saying "….for the period of….", it will say "….as of…" a particular date.

Another way to think about it is this: Once you are working and earning a paycheck and paying bills on your household, your cash balance in a checking account is just an ongoing balance. The balance will ebb and flow over your lifetime, but the amount of cash you have on hand at any given moment is "as of" that date. The same situation exists for a company and its balance sheet.

Another example: we as individuals may own a home and have a mortgage that we are paying off over 20–30 years. The house will be a long-term asset to us, just like if a company buys a building. We both will carry that asset on our balance sheet for as long as we own that asset. Plus, over time, we will be paying off that long-term liability on the balance sheet.

Think of it this way, if this helps: The balance sheet carries **all** the financial decisions the company has made over its entire life as a company. You may even hear people talk about why they prefer certain financial statements over others. Personally, all of the financial statements should be a concern in understanding how they work together. However, you can make your own decisions about which one carries more weight in your analysis as you build your financial acumen!

Translating This Information

As you are reading this section, remember that we have the same financial information in managing our household as individuals. Instead of calling it a **balance sheet**, we will call it a **net worth statement**. Thus, anytime you hear anyone talking about their net worth, you now know that they are talking about their balance sheet!

A company will have **ASSETS**, and an individual will have **ASSETS**. For a company, this can be buildings, cars, trucks (like delivery vehicles), land, equipment, cash, inventory, etc[3]. An individual can have similar items, but we typically have vehicles, a house, investments in securities or other financial instruments, land, jewelry, and other items.

In addition, for a company and an individual, you will have **LIABILITIES**[4]. For a company, their liabilities could include several things – they could have mortgages on buildings, they could have issued bonds to generate cash, but the bonds have to be paid back, and they have bills to pay just like an individual does. For an individual, we will have credit card balances to pay, vendors to pay, mortgages to pay, etc.

The only difference between a company and an individual is the difference between **EQUITY** and **NET WORTH**[5]. These sections of the balance sheet essentially represent the same thing. The net worth is essentially the equity we have built in our household, but we call it net worth instead of equity.

Topic 8: Short Term versus Long Term

You will notice that there are time distinctions of short term (current) and long term on the balance sheet. Generally, speaking accountants use a one-year time frame to determine short-term assets and liabilities. Thus, when you think about this, you are thinking about "how quickly can this asset be turned into cash"? Accountants use a one-year time frame to identify if an asset is a short-term asset[6].

If we apply this rule to the cash account on the balance sheet, cash is already in the form of cash. Thus, cash is the "most liquid" asset that a company has, and that is why it is listed first on every balance sheet you will ever examine.

Then, usually, what you will see listed second on the balance sheet is accounts receivable. Accounts receivable will generally be turned into cash in a short amount of time, and it will depend on credit terms that a company gives to suppliers. Thus, if a company says to Customer A based on your credit rating, we will provide you with terms of paying your invoices within 30 days. If they tell Customer B, you can pay your invoices within 45 days, and if your customers take the full amount of days to pay, then when you average the data out, the invoices would turn into cash much faster than a one-year time frame. As you are examining a company's balance sheet, the short-term assets will be listed in the order of how fast they can be turned into cash.

Beyond the one-year time frame, you will have long-term assets[7]. The most common long-term assets a company will have are the assets that will exist for over one year and are often not turned into cash, but they often generate cash. One of the most common assets in this category is the "property, plant and equipment" or "fixed assets." This category on the balance sheet represents things like machinery that are used in production. A machine used in production might be on the balance sheet for 10 years, 20 years, 30 years, or longer. It is because of that time frame that the asset will be classified as a long-term asset.

The same framework is used for liabilities on the balance sheet. Often, the most common short-term liability that you will see on the balance sheet is accounts payable. This account represents the amount of money that has to be spent with suppliers. For example, your company will be a customer of other companies. Those companies will sell products to you, and you may be given terms like 30 days to pay invoices to them. Thus, you want to think about them in terms of how long it takes to use the cash for liabilities. For accounts payable, this will be a time frame shorter than one year.

These accounts will often represent the debt obligations that a company has to pay over a longer time frame than one year for long-term liabilities. For example, a company can take out a loan with the bank to be paid back over five years, or a company can take out a mortgage to pay for a production facility to be paid back over 20 or 30 years, or a company can issue bonds that have to be repaid over a long period of time.

Topic 9: Assets

The balance sheet is called the "balance sheet" because it MUST balance. There are three major sections to the balance sheet: assets, liabilities, and equity. This is also known as the **accounting equation,** which is represented by the following equation:

Assets = Liabilities + Equity

In this section, you will learn even more about how to assess assets, liabilities, and equity on the balance sheet.

Current Asset: Cash

Cash should be straightforward to understand because it represents the cash that a company has in the bank. However, there is also another term called "Cash Equivalents." Cash equivalents represent investments that the company could turn into cash within a few hours or within a day[8]. Another way to think about cash equivalents is how "liquid" they are, which means how quickly they can turn into cash.

Using this conversion idea, the ability to turn an asset into cash, the cash is the company's most liquid asset. In addition, cash equivalents can be turned into cash so quickly they are often listed together on a balance sheet.

A cash equivalent can be a deposit certificate, a treasury bill issued by the U.S. government, or money market funds. These investment types can be turned into cash in a very short period of time, thus making them a cash equivalent. These are the safer investments where a company can use cash to earn a modest return on the cash while having the flexibility to pull the money back into cash to use for operations or other investments.

Current Asset: Accounts Receivable

All the current assets are listed in the order of how liquid they are or how quickly the asset can be turned into cash. Generally, the second item you will see on the balance sheet in the current assets section will be **accounts receivable**. Accounts receivable represent the sales of the company that has not been turned into cash[9].

You have already learned what accounts receivable represents on the balance sheet. Now, you want to know how the company is managing that asset. There are a couple of ways that you can assess how well accounts receivable is managed.

One of the ways is to look at the aging of the accounts receivable. In most accounting software, this is one of the common reports that can be run. The report will list all the customer's open invoices and let you know if the invoice is 30 days old, 60 days old, 120 days old, or older. Accounting software will often allow you to determine the days of the categories, but these are common groupings. The important thing here is that you want all of your invoices to be within current terms for the customer. Thus, if you have given a customer 30 days to pay, you do not want to see that invoice NOT PAID on day 35 after the invoice was generated.

Typical accounts receivable aging report would look something like this (Figure 9):

| | | A/R Aging Summary | | | | | | |
| | | As of June 21, 2021 | | | | | | |
	Current	1-30 days	31-60 days	61-90 days	91 -120 days	>120 days	Total	
Customer 1		$ 300.00					$ 300.00	
Customer 2			$ 200.00				$ 200.00	
Customer 3	$ 600.00						$ 600.00	
Customer 4		$ 150.00	$ 100.00		$ 400.00		$ 650.00	
Total	$ 600.00	$ 450.00	$ 300.00	$ -	$ 400.00	$ -	$ 1,750.00	

Figure 9   Sample A/R Aging Summary

One thing to note, some small businesses may run on credit card transactions for the most part. In that case, you may not see a lot of accounts receivable balances that are open. For instance, suppose that you are a business that produces an online software product, and you charge a yearly subscription for the software. You will likely have credit card information stored in your system, and you will charge that credit card each year. When a credit card is charged, you may send the customer an invoice, but you have already charged the credit card. There will be no need to be watching accounts receivable balances. In this case, you want to know how many people keep their subscription over time and how many people request refunds on their subscription.

Current Asset: Inventory

Inventory is a current asset, but inventory can often turn slower into cash than other current assets[10]. One thing to make sure that you understand is that there can be different kinds of inventory accounts.

One type of inventory is called **raw materials inventory**. Raw materials are the ingredients that are used in manufacturing or assembling a product[11]. The raw materials will sit in the inventory until they are pulled to manufacture or assemble a product. So, if you are a company that builds computers, you would buy all of the individual components and have them in your raw material inventory until you pull parts to build a computer.

Then, when the raw materials are pulled for the manufacture or assembly process, the inventory is transferred into **work in process** type of inventory account. Thus, even if the production process only takes ten minutes or if it takes several days, the materials will sit in that account until the product is manufactured or assembled. While working on assembling a computer, the parts will be in work in process inventory until the computer is built.

Once a production or assembly job completes, the materials now are transformed into a new product, and a **finished good** is called a computer[12]. This finished good will also have labor costs included for the assembly, and the computer will now be waiting to be moved to a retail store inventory (if you have a store presence) and to be sold to a customer.

In addition to these inventories, you may also have an accessories inventory. You may also want to sell accessories like separate keyboards, mice, mousepads, and other items that you buy directly at a bulk or warehouse direct discount and sell to customers. These products you buy, mark them up and sell them directly to customers.

Depending on the size of the computer manufacturing and assembly, you may have some automated manufacturing. Thus, you may need some spare parts for these machines. The spare parts inventory is not something sold to the customer, and it is for the assembly process only. Thus, this is a specific inventory that has not ever turned into cash, this type of inventory is only a use of cash. Suppose you are examining a business for purchase or expansion of your current business. In that case, you may want to make sure that you ask about the size of this inventory and how well it is being managed and take out the effect of this inventory on the days sales outstanding and inventory turnover ratios.

The key to the turnover metrics on your inventory is to ensure that your inventory is being purchased, converted into a finished good, and then sold as quickly as possible. This turnover rate by product category, or specific product, can tell you a great deal about how efficiently you are managing your inventory.

Think about it this way, suppose a company has $100,000 average inventory, and the cost of goods sold of products is $600,000. In this case, your inventory, IN TOTAL, is moving six times a year ($600,000 / $100,000). Thus, every two months, you are turning all of your inventory into cash.

However, are all the product categories moving among all your products included in the inventory at the same rate? Can we say for sure that all inventory is turned at this rate? No, you cannot say that. To better understand the efficiency, you hopefully can use this same formula and capture the turnover rate of every single item or group of items.

For example, you could have some products moving very slowly and some products moving very fast. What if you found that some products were moving very slow? There could be a few reasons for this. One reason could be that you have products in inventory that you no longer sell. Another reason could be that you just bought too much at one time of certain products that are just not moving as fast.

Often, software today can help you do this analysis, but not every software program may have this capability. However, a good accountant can help you with these calculations and help develop a process by which you can assess turnover. The important thing to remember is that cash is tied up in inventory, so staying on top of turnover makes the operations more efficient. Plus, if you start having inventory that is not used anymore, you can figure out if a donation needs to be made or sell the items for a little bit of money back to the company.

Sometimes the inventory that does not move will meet an expiration date. For example, grocery products and other food items can have an expiration date where all you can do is perhaps write off that inventory. The key to managing this type of inventory is making sure that you have good, solid prediction formulas to help you keep just the right amount of inventory on hand.

Otherwise, the other culprit of extending inventory turnover is obsolete items. **Obsolete inventory** is the inventory that no longer has a useful application in your business[13]. For instance, you may have parts for a machine you no longer use. An important part of managing inventory will be keeping a list of parts associated with its "parent." Thus, if you make personal computers if you have a particular part that makes "Laptop X" – like a particular hard drive-you want to make sure that Laptop X and that hard drive are associated. Thus, if you STOP producing Laptop X, then you can assess all of the parts that made that went into producing that laptop. That way, if you can re-use those parts on another laptop, then great, otherwise, you can get that inventory out of your storage to make way for other inventory, and you might even get a little of your money back if you can sell it, or scrap it, and worse case is you give it away.

Long-Term Asset: Property, Plant, and Equipment

Often, the largest long-term asset of a company is the account called "**Property, Plant and Equipment**," or you can also see this called "Fixed Assets." These are assets that are never sold to the customer, but they often assist in generating cash[14]. Any production and warehousing equipment or buildings that will house production and warehousing equipment have the purpose of generating products for sale.

For example, suppose a machine that you buy is worth several hundred thousand dollars that help you automate a part of the manufacturing process of building a computer. In that case, you will capture the value of that machine in a fixed assets account on the balance sheet. Thus, many people who study the financial statements of different companies look at the return on assets financial ratio.

Depreciation

Depreciation is an accounting procedure that allows you to recognize the expense of investment into buildings or machinery, or other assets on your income statement over time[15]. For example, if you are investing in a piece of machinery worth $500,000, you can depreciate that asset over its useful life. Perhaps your fixed assets person or your CPA will determine that the asset's useful life is 20 years, and your CPA expects that the value of the piece of machinery will only be $20,000 after the 20 years of use.

Before getting into the mechanism of depreciation calculations, think about why this mechanism exists. One reason for this is that

$500,000 is a considerable expense to hit the income statement all at once. Think about the price tag of purchasing or constructing a building. The price tag could be millions of dollars, so that would be a significant impact on your income statement in one period.

Secondly, depreciation expense is connected to the "accumulated depreciation" on the balance sheet. The accumulated depreciation account offsets the asset's original purchase price so that you always know the "book value" of the asset[16].

There are several different methods by which a fixed assets accountant would spread the depreciation expense over the asset's life, but the simplest way to do it is to approach it by the straight-line method[17]. This method means is that we will take the original purchase price minus the salvage value divided by the asset's life

In our example, then, the formula would look like this:

Original Purchase
Price $500,000
Useful Life 20 years
Salvage Value $20,000
$$= (\$500,000 - \$20,000)/(20 \text{ years} \times 12 \text{ months})$$
$$= \$480,000/240 \text{ months}$$
$$= \$2,000 \text{ depreciation expense/month}$$

Thus, over time, each month, the company will record a depreciation expense of $2,000 with an offset of a corresponding $2,000 credit in accumulated depreciation. Over time, over the 240 months, the accumulated depreciation account will eventually have accumulated $480,000, and the original purchase price of $500,000 will still be on the balance sheet as an asset. The net value, or the salvage value, at month 241 will be $500,000–$480,000 = $20,000.

The asset could be disposed of or sold before that 240th month or after, and the proceeds would be compared with whatever the difference is between the original purchase price and the accumulated depreciation. More importantly, though, the depreciation expense, to reiterate, is NOT PAID to any government agency. Thus, this is an accounting entry to help the business keep a book value of assets, but this is a NON-CASH entry.

Amortization

Amortization is an accounting procedure that allows you to recognize the expense of investment into non-tangible assets on your
income statement over time[18]. The idea is the same as depreciation,
and it is just that this procedure is being applied to something like
goodwill or even to software licensing. Goodwill is often the difference in the purchase price of a business acquisition and the value of
the business acquisition. Licensing can be very expensive, but the
license is intangible. Every company will have a policy or practice
that establishes a threshold of how much total cost can be expensed to
the income statement or capitalized as a project and then amortized
over time. For some companies, this could be $20,000, or $100,000,
or more[19] (see also Part Two, Deeper Dive into Cost of Goods Sold).

For example, in one company I worked for, the information technology department had an interesting rule and terminology for this
idea. It may be something that you may hear of in your career. In
this company, they had a cutoff of $300K, and if the cost of a proj-
ect went above this number, then the project would be capitalized
and amortized. The project may be amortized for 10 years up to 30
years, depending on how long they assessed the life of the technology asset.

In addition, the company called money spent below the $300K
mark to be "hard" money, meaning that the money would all impact
the income statement as incurred. A project over $300K was consid-
ered "soft" money, meaning that the impact to the income statement
would be spread over a much longer period of time.

Another nuance to this idea is how human resources are used in
an information technology department. For example, if you have
an information technology department that has a mix of full-time
direct employees and you also employ various consulting companies, which resources would you consider using for a capitalized
(soft money) project versus a non-capitalized (hard money) project? Consulting resources tend to be more expensive than full-time
direct employees (even with benefits added). A company may very
well be more heavily weighted to outside consulting resources for
soft money projects.

Topic 10: Liabilities

In this section, you will learn even more about the liabilities recorded on the balance sheet. Liabilities will also be classified as current (short-term) and long-term liabilities.

Current Liability: Accounts Payable

Accounts payable most often will represent the amounts owed to suppliers[20]. Every month, as a business is operating, the company is incurring costs. There are various types of costs: buying parts from suppliers, paying contractors and services vendors, paying rents, paying for insurance, and possibly paying benefits for employees, just to name a few!

From a processing perspective, a company will often set up purchase orders for products and services. Not all companies do this, but if a company is publicly traded, they will do it this way. The nice thing about purchase orders is that the creation sets up many default information about future transactions. One of the default pieces of information will be an account number representing the expense account or another type of account, where the charges will be processed when the products and services are received.

So, what does this mean for you? Well, in many IT departments, you will be potentially managing a budget. Thus, you could have a line item for some type of monthly expense, perhaps for a maintenance contract. When the purchase order was set up, the account number was set at that time.

What if your department merges with another department? The account number that defaults on the purchase order will not change just because there was a reorganization within the company. Therefore, many managers have been frustrated because their budget details have line items that are going to the wrong accounts. Now you know that to fix that, you need to go to the purchasing or accounts payable department to fix the source of the problem!

Many of the coding issues will have a source in the accounting department, so the key is to know for any particular account on the profit and loss statement or the balance sheet to identify the SOURCE of information for that account. For example, use the revenue account as an example. Revenue represents sales of the business of products and services. So, where are the sources of information about revenue?

The source document will usually be an invoice that is created. The source may not always be an invoice, but it is a place to start. However, that invoice will have certain default information associated with it. When the customer is entered into the system, there could be a default revenue account that is associated with the customer. Or the products and services could drive the revenue account that is the default. Thus, if the business has restructured, a customer may belong in a different department, you would have to make sure that any default accounts are restructured.

In addition, some businesses may not have revenue driven by invoices. Some or all revenue could be driven by credit card transactions or direct payments to a bank account. Thus, the transaction may be accounted for by an accountant or by a journal entry.

The challenge you may have is knowing how to find that source of data, but it is important to identify and document where the source of data is so that you can fix errors at the source. For those of you that may be involved in budgeting, and the sources of data in budgets should be part of the budget development. You will save an enormous amount of time and be much more efficient and thus relates to savings of time and money for your department!

In terms of accounts payable, everything will go back to either the customer record in the system or the products and services that are purchased on purchase orders. Thus, the same logic applies to make sure and document where the source of the data is in your budget. And small businesses could just have expenses coming through the bank account by debit card purchases or bank transfers. Thus, the accountant or bookkeeper may be coding those entries. A lot of software today can build default account numbers for recurring transactions, and therefore that would be the source of the error if errors start showing up in your books.

Long-Term Liabilities

Long-term liabilities are those debts that are paid over more than a year[21]. Another way that a company may refer to these long-term liabilities is by the nomenclature of "noncurrent" liabilities or "long-term debt."

A company could raise cash by issuing a bond to the public. An investor can then invest in that bond, but it is a liability that the company must pay back to the investors. Bonds can be issued for a year or up to 30 years. Now, any part of a bond that is owed within one year will be classified as a short-term liability, but the remaining liability amount will be listed as long-term liabilities.

For example, you could be paying a $1 million loan over 30 years, and the first year of the 30-year loan will be considered a CURRENT liability, and the rest of the long-term liability would be in the long-term liability section. Every year of the long-term liability would get reclassified this way, so it is important to watch for this when examining the liabilities section[22].

A company can also have other types of long-term liabilities on its books. The company can enter into long-term loans with a bank, possibly have a mortgage on physical buildings, and other types of long-term debt that are repaid over a long period of time.

Topic 11: Equity

In this section, you will learn even more about the equity section of the balance sheet. Equity is the net worth of a company, just like an individual can build up his or her net worth[23]. There are two major categories of accounts that are within this section on the balance sheet.

Stock   For a company that is publicly traded, you will see various types of stock accounts in the equity section. The most common type of stock is "**common stock**," and it is this type of stock that is sold on the major exchanges in the United States (like the New York Stock Exchange or the NASDAQ)[24]. Issuing stock is a great way to raise cash for a company.

Retained Earnings

The **retained earnings** balance represents the profits or losses the company has incurred over time[25]. A common question that is asked is, but wait, are the profits and losses recorded on the income statement? The answer to that is YES, they are. However, the income statement represents the profit or loss for one period of time.

Let us explore what this means. Assume that a company works on a reporting period of a calendar month. Each month, during the closing of the books that accountants do in the company, the accounting software will clear out the balances in all the revenue accounts and the expense accounts on the income statement and move those balances to the retained earnings account. Thus, every accounting period, the income statement "starts over" with zero balances in the revenue and expense accounts.

Therefore, when you assess the retained earnings balance, you are looking at profits and losses for the company over the life of that company. What you want to see is a healthy generation of equity built up in the company.

In addition, the equity section of a balance sheet of a publicly traded company will also have different types of stock that have been issued. Most commonly, common stock will be listed in this section. **Common stock** is the stock that is offered to the general public through trading exchanges.

Part Three: What to Watch Out For

- Balance sheets must balance. Assets = Liabilities + Equity.
- Cash, accounts receivable, inventory, and accounts payable are considered the working capital of the company.
- Inventory could be turned into cash a lot slower than other current assets like accounts receivable.
- Cash equivalents can be turned into cash very quickly.
- Long-term liabilities should have a current liability amount for the year that is being paid off in the current year.

Part Three: Exercises, Practice, and Resources

Learning activities:

1. In the 10-k, can you find information on short-term versus long-term assets and liabilities? Does the 10-k give you any information on how these are calculated?

2. Can you find any information on the different kinds of inventory accounts that are in use in the company? Remember, the inventory listed is a consolidated number and can represent all kinds of different inventory accounts.

3. Does the company have cash equivalents? What does that represent for the company?

4. Are you able to get your hands on an accounts receivable aging schedule?

5. Are you able to get your hands on an accounts payable aging schedule?

6. If a company does have different kinds of inventory, look to calculate turnover rates on the different types of inventory.

7. If you work for the company you are studying, ask to see the aging of the accounts receivable balances.

8. If you are assessing a company for possible purchase, if the company does not have aging of accounts receivable, as for a report to be created or an accountant help build this report for you.

9. If the company has fixed assets (i.e., property, plant, and equipment), can you find out what makes up this balance? Is it raw land? Is it buildings? Fleets of cars? How are they depreciated?

10. How much depreciation expense is deducted every year for these assets (property, plant, and equipment)?

11. Does the company have technology assets that are being amortized? Can you find solid reasons why some assets are depreciated and which assets are amortized?

12. Pull at least five years (more if you have access to more years) of balance sheets. Are the accounts growing? Are liabilities growing faster than equity? Is there steady growth in numbers, or does each year show a lot of variation? Use the

principles of horizontal analysis in Topic 20 of this book to prepare the calculations.

13. What kinds of long-term liabilities does the company have? What were they investing in for the liabilities?

14. How do retained earnings look? Is it showing many periods of gains or losses?

15. Most often, you may be comparing year over year. However, you can also compare quarter to quarter, or first quarter to first quarter, or second quarter to second quarter. Different ways of slicing the data can give you specific insights!

16. At this juncture in your study, which company is performing best? You can include both the income statement and balance sheet in your assessment overall.

17. Assess hard and soft money projects. Examine how a company utilizes amortization.

Notes

1 What is the balance sheet? Retrieved from https://corporatefinanceinstitute. com/resources/knowledge/accounting/balance-sheet/

2 What is the accounting equation? Retrieved from https:// corporatefinanceinstitute.com/resources/knowledge/accounting/ accounting-equation/

3 What are the main types of assets? Retrieved from https://corporatefi-nanceinstitute.com/resources/knowledge/accounting/types-of-assets/

4 What are the main types of liabilities? Retrieved from https://corpo-ratefinanceinstitute.com/resources/knowledge/accounting/types-of-liabilities/

5 Shareholder equity vs. net worth – Top 5 differences you should know. Retrieved from https://www.wallstreetmojo.com/shareholder-equity-vs-net-worth/

6 Short-term asset definition. Retrieved from https://www.accounting-tools.com/articles/what-is-a-short-term-asset.html

7 What is a long-term asset? Retrieved from https://www.accountingcoach. com/blog/what-is-a-long-term-asset

8 What are cash equivalents? Retrieved from https://corporatefinancein-stitute.com/resources/knowledge/accounting/cash-equivalents/

9 Accounts payable versus accounts receivable. Retrieved from https://cor-poratefinanceinstitute.com/resources/knowledge/accounting/ accounts-payable-vs-accounts-receivable/

10 What is inventory? Types, examples, and analysis (2020). Retrieved from https://www.netsuite.com/portal/resource/articles/inventory-management/inventory.shtml

11 Raw materials inventory definition. Retrieved from https://www.accountingtools.com/articles/2017/5/13/raw-materials-inventory#:~:text=Raw%20materials%20inventory%20is%20the,process%20or%20finished%20goods%20production.&text=These%20are%20materials%20not%20incorporated,consumed%20during%20the%20production%20process.

12 Finished goods inventory: formula, calculation, and turnover. Retrieved from https://www.bluecart.com/blog/finished-goods-inventory

13 What is obsolete inventory? Retrieved from https://www.accountingcoach.com/blog/what-is-obsolete-inventory

14 PP&E (Property, Plant and Equipment). Retrieved from https://corporatefinanceinstitute.com/resources/knowledge/accounting/ppe-property-plant-equipment/

15 What is depreciation and how to calculate it (2020). Retrieved from https://bench.co/blog/tax-tips/depreciation/

16 Accumulated depreciation. Retrieved from https://corporatefinanceinstitute.com/resources/knowledge/accounting/accumulated-depreciation/

17 Straight line depreciation. Retrieved from https://corporatefinanceinstitute.com/resources/knowledge/accounting/straight-line-depreciation/

18 Amortization. Retrieved from https://corporatefinanceinstitute.com/resources/knowledge/accounting/amortization/

19 Wehner, C. (n.d.). Accounting for Computer Software Costs. Retrieved from https://www.gma-cpa.com/blog/accounting-for-computer-software-costs

20 Accounts payable. Retrieved from https://www.accountingcoach.com/accounts-payable/explanation

21 Accounting 101 basics of long term liability. Retrieved from https://smallbusiness.chron.com/accounting-101-basics-long-term-liability-60869.html

22 Halton, C. (2020). Current Portion of Long-Term Debt (CPLTD). Retrieved from https://www.investopedia.com/terms/c/currentportion-longtermdebt.asp

23 Stockholders Equity. Retrieved from https://corporatefinanceinstitute.com/resources/knowledge/accounting/stockholders-equity-guide/

24 What is common stock? Retrieved from https://www.thebalance.com/common-stocks-3305892

25 Retained earnings. Retrieved from https://corporatefinanceinstitute.com/resources/knowledge/accounting/retained-earnings-guide/

PART FOUR
CASH FLOW STATEMENTS

A **cash flow statement** shows how the cash balance is changing in your business[1]. For publicly traded companies who are required to use the accrual basis of accounting, or for any other business that elects to use accrual-based accounting, you now know that this means a company is recognizing cash inflow and cash outflow before the cash is exchanged. Thus, a cash flow statement is a reconciliation of the cash to the accrual-based accounting system.

A cash flow statement is based on how cash is GENERATED or USED in the business. When you look at a cash flow statement, there are three sections:

1. Cash generated or used from operations
2. Cash generated or used from investing
3. Cash generated or used from financing

Many small businesses are based on the cash basis of accounting, and therefore, the cash flow does not need to be reconciled at all. But this assumes that ALL transactions, as they come in and out of your bank account, are being coded to revenue or expense accounts. If, for some reason, they are not being coded to revenue and expense, but are coded to balance sheet accounts, then you may have a need for a cash flow statement.

Most software today will create a cash flow statement. If you are studying a publicly traded business, then the cash flow statement is available to you in the 10-k. If you are analyzing a business to purchase, you would have to learn how to create a cash flow statement or have an accounting professional help prepare a cash flow statement. If the company you are analyzing is on QuickBooks or some other software type, the company can likely prepare that cash flow statement.

DOI: 10.1201/9781003110613-4   **65**

The important thing to remember is that cash flow is truly focused on the additions and subtractions from the cash balance. This approach is different than the income statement that is recognizing revenue and expenses in the period incurred. A publicly traded company has to follow specific rules about revenue and expense recognition; the profits are estimated and do not reflect actual cash gained or spent.

Topic 12: How Profit and Cash Are Related to Financial Statements

Throughout the book, the idea that profit and cash are not the same has been pointed out several times. Now that you are aware of this, and we have talked through different accounts on the profit and loss statement and the balance sheet, we will summarize information using the information you have learned before.

In the profit and loss statement, a company is generating or using cash to generate profits. Thus, revenue generation is a cash generation activity. You now know that the cash for the revenue can generate before, at the same time, or after the revenue recognition occurred.

The cost of goods sold is cash used to generate the profits on the sale of products and services. Gross profit then shows you the net profits generated from the revenue minus the cost of goods sold.

From the gross profit, you will have operating expenses, representing the cash being used to run the rest of the company. These expenses occur regardless of if there is a sale or not of goods and services.

Eventually, a company will have a net profit (hopefully). This amount of money is cleared OUT of the profit and loss statement and into the equity section of the balance sheet. The clearing out process means that every revenue account, every cost of goods sold account, and every expense account is reduced to zero, and the summarized amounts go into the retained earnings account in the equity section of the balance sheet.

Thus, on the balance sheet, the retained earnings represent the company's profits over the company's life.

In addition, asset accounts and liabilities accounts will change over time. For example, in one reporting period, the accounts receivable balance might be $100,000, and in the next reporting period, the accounts receivable balance could be higher or lower than the month before. Suppose the accounts receivable balance went up to $150,000 (from $100,000 the period before). In that case, this could mean an increase in credit sales and that the company is having a more challenging time turning their accounts receivable into cash. Either way, this movement of the balances means that accounts receivable has "used" cash from the previous period.

If the accounts receivable balance went down to $50,000 (from $100,000 the period before), then this could mean that more accounts receivable has been successfully converted to cash and that credit sales have gone down. In this case, the accounts receivable balance has "generated" cash.

Each of the cash flow statement sections will reflect how cash was "generated" or "used" in the business. Plus, you want to view the cash flow statement as a "reconciliation" of the cash account on the balance sheet. Thus, the beginning cash and the ending cash balance should be the same number that can be found on the cash balance of the balance sheet.

Topic 13: Operating, Financing, and Investing Activities

A cash flow statement shows you how the cash balance is changing through three different activities that a business can engage in: operations, investing, and financing. Another way you can think about this statement is to reconcile the cash account on the balance sheet by showing the additions and subtractions of cash and if those additions and subtractions are associated with different general ledger accounts categorized as operations, financing, and investing.

Cash Generated or Used from Operating Activities

In a company, cash is either being "generated" or "used." Within the **operations activities** of the business, you generate cash through sales of products and services, and you use money by paying bills. Therefore, a profit and loss statement can often be called a "Statement of Operations."

Now, one item that you will often see in this section of the cash flow statement is an item called "depreciation and amortization." This line item is always "added back" into the cash. The reason it is added back in is that any depreciation expense or amortization expense, when deducted as an expense on the income statement, is a NON-CASH expense. In other words, there is NO payment to a vendor for this expense.

When we pay utilities, there is a transfer of money from the company to the vendor. When we pay rent, there is a transfer of funds from the company to the vendor, but there is no agency or company that you are paying in the case of depreciation and amortization. Thus, that money must be added BACK to the cash balance because the money never left the bank account.

In addition, it is essential to note that your working capital accounts will also be listed here on the balance sheet – accounts like accounts receivable, inventory, and accounts payable. The reason for this is because these accounts are considered to "operating" assets and liabilities.

That makes sense if you think about it logically. Why do accounts receivable exist in the first place? It exists because sometimes, when you have a revenue-generating event, you have not received the cash yet from the customer. Or, if you have recognized a bill you have to pay in accounts payable, you may not have sent the bank transfer yet for the expense. Likewise, you can have inventory sit on your books for quite a while before a sales transaction occurs.

What you want to look for in this cash flow section is that more cash is being generated by the business than cash that is being used in the business. Operations is where most of the "generated" cash flow will come from in a company. Or, at the very least, net cash generation will hopefully be a consistent level.

Cash Generated or Used from Investing Activities

Another section you will find on cash flow statements is devoted to **investing activities**. Investing for companies can be through areas like investing in securities or the purchasing of equipment. Most of the time, you will see net "uses" of cash here, but it can fluctuate quite a bit depending on the company's decisions about where they put their cash for returns.

These tend to be longer-term investments. For example, a company could buy bonds of other companies or municipalities to generate interest payments as other income sources or invest in treasury bills. These are often "safer" investments that are not speculative in nature but can provide a little more significant rate of return than parking all the cash in a bank savings account.

This section also includes cash being generated or used by investing in capital expenditures. Capital expenditures correlate to the discussion of depreciation and amortization in the long-term liabilities section of the book. The company may be using some of its cash on hand to buy property, plant, equipment, purchase a business, or invest in information technology. Those investments, when capitalized, will be reflected in this section. Generally speaking, you may see more "uses" of cash in this section of the cash flow statement.

Cash Generated or Used from Financing Activities

Another section on the cash flow statement has to do with **financing activities**. Here a company can generate cash through borrowing activities (think of loans), issuing their own bonds to the public, or by issuing common stock to the public. Borrowing money generates a debt obligation for the company (liability) while issuing common stock is shareholder-focused (equity). Payment of a dividend (a payment made of holders of stock) is a use of cash in this section as well. Generally speaking, you may see more "uses" of cash in this section of the cash flow statement.

Topic 14: How All Financial Statements Fit Together

The financial statements are related. However, as you have read through the material so far and worked on various activities, you may not have picked up on the connections. Here you will examine **how** these financial statements are related.

Income Statement to Balance Sheet

Revenue to Assets Revenue events are the sales events of the business. In some cases, you are obtaining cash when the sale happens, and in other cases, you are setting up a receivable where your business will be paid later. Either way, revenue equates to the assets section of the balance sheet (see Figure 10 below).

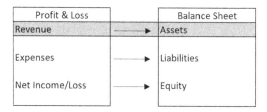

Figure 10   Revenue to Assets

Expenses to Liabilities Expenses that are paid or recognized on the profit and loss statement are paying for short-term and long-term liabilities on the balance sheet. Thus, if an expense is recognized, it may not have been paid yet. Therefore, this is why there is a relationship between the expenses and the liabilities (see Figure 11 below).

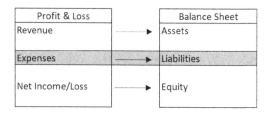

Figure 11   Expenses to Liabilities

Net Income to Equity The income statement and the balance sheet are related to how the accounting world manages the estimated profit and loss every month. In accounting software, every month, the income statement accounts are "swept" to the balance sheet. You do not need to know how this happens; all you need to know is that it DOES happen (see Figure 9 below). The more you see the interplay of the accounts on the different financial statements, the higher your financial intelligence will be! (Figure 12)

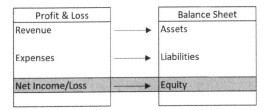

Figure 12   Net Income to Equity

Every account on the profit and loss statement is reduced to zero at the end of an accounting period so that the new accounting period can start with a zero balance for the profit and loss accounts. For example, if you had $100K in revenue in Period One, that $100K does NOT carry over to the next reporting period. Thus, every revenue account, every expense account, "starts over" at the beginning of the next accounting period.

Thus, all the accounts are reduced to zero, and the balances are moved to the balance sheet. On the balance sheet, these amounts are transferred to the retained earnings account in the equity section of the balance sheet. Thus, the retained earnings account is a collection of ALL the net profits and net losses over the business's life. Think of it this way, if it helps: All the estimated profits and losses from OPERATIONS go to the retained earnings.

An important observation is to be made here; as you can see in the previous diagrams, the profit and loss statement and the balance sheet line up perfectly to one another in terms of the interplay of the accounts represented on each financial statement. You may be thinking, if revenue is related to assets, and expenses relate to liabilities, then why would you have to transfer the not profit and loss to the equity section of the balance sheet?

The answer to this is fairly simplified, but it may take a while to dawn on you. But the answer boils down to the fact that the profit and loss *calculates* a profit or loss. In addition, remember back to Parts Two and Three of this book, where we discussed that a profit and loss statement is prepared FOR a specific period of time; thus, the balances do NOT accumulate, and the balance sheet accounts ARE an accumulation over time. So, since the profit and loss statement is a calculation of the net profit or loss, in order to start over for the next reporting period, which calculated profit and loss has to be moved by a journal entry to the equity section of the balance sheet.

Income Statement to Cash Flow Statement

Generally, the income statement is revenue minus expenses equal to net profit or loss. However, if we examine the smaller details of a profit and loss statement, we see some distinct sections. Each of those sections relates to the cash flow statement in a direct way (Figure 13).

Profit & Loss
Revenue
- Cost of Goods Sold
= Gross Profit
- Operating Expenses
= EBITDA
- Depreciation
- Amortization
= EBIT
- Interest
- Income Taxes
Net Income/Loss

Figure 13   Detailed Sections of Profit and Loss

In Figure 12, you see that revenue will have a corresponding cost of goods sold (sometimes called cost of revenue) being subtracted. These are the direct costs of producing your products or services. The revenue minus cost of goods sold will then give you a calculated gross profit. Then, you will have operating expenses subtracted from gross profit, which will give you a calculated earnings before interest, taxes, depreciation, and amortization (EBITDA)[2]. This can also be called operating income.

Then, you have a section where depreciation and amortization are being deducted, and then you have interest and taxes being deducted. Not every single profit and loss statement will look exactly like this, so you need to know how these different accounts translate to the cash flow statement.

Therefore, you will want to refer to this figure for more detail on the connect (Figure 14):

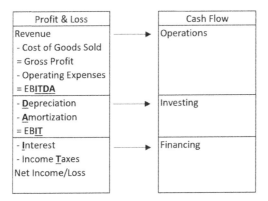

Figure 14   Income Statement to Cash Flow

Thus, when you look at the income statement, the revenue to operating expenses represents activities generated within your company's operations. These accounts directly translate to the operations section of the cash flow statement. For example, since revenue can generate accounts receivable, you will see changes in the accounts receivable balance in the operations section of the cash flow statement.

The depreciation and amortization expenses are related to investing activities. The reason for these accounts is that your company could be investing in long-term assets like buildings, land, equipment, expense computers, and technology infrastructure. All of those assets can be depreciated or amortized to track the book value of those assets. Thus, you are "investing" some of your cash reserves into those assets.

Finally, when your company pays interest, it is because the company is paying interest on a bond issue. Those bonds are a debt to the organization, and you must pay interest to the investors that invest in those bonds. That is why this section of the income statement relates to the "financing" section of the cash flow statement. Any time you issue bonds, which is a financing, or debt, activity.

Balance Sheet to Cash Flow Statement

The balance sheet is a bit trickier when it comes to translating how these accounts translate to the cash flow statement. However, we will work with this figure to explain the connections (Figure 15):

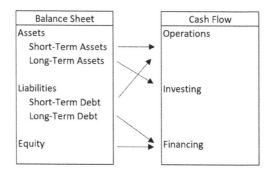

Figure 15   Balance Sheet to Cash Flow Statement

The first thing to make sure you understand is the idea of "short-term." For example, a short-term liability account is Accounts Payable. Because it is short-term in nature, meaning that payment is due within 30 days, 90 days, or anything else shorter than a one-year time frame, we are talking about the business's operations. Short-term assets are things like cash, accounts receivable, and inventory accounts. All of these accounts have to do with operating the business in the short term. Thus, any account in the "short-term" sections of the balance sheet (whether in assets or liabilities) will be considered part of the business's operations and directly translate to that section in the cash flow statement. The balance sheet will categorize the short-term accounts and the long-term accounts, so they should not be hard to find!

Long-Term assets are an investment a company makes that will often be paid over terms that are much greater than a year. A Chief Financial Officer (CFO) may have preferences about how much cash versus how much money the company is willing to borrow to acquire or build an asset.

Topic 15: Working Capital Management

Working capital management is a phrase you may hear from time to time[3]. Working capital is about the cash generated and used in the business in the short term. Another way to think about this is that working capital management is how a company ensures that they have the cash for operating activities[4].

Working capital management is the strategy a company uses to manage inventory and accounts receivable assets and the liability of accounts payable. Each requires different strategies, but the focus is to generate cash AS FAST as you can and HOLD ON to cash for as long as possible.

While employees and investors may not be too concerned with the day-to-day operational details of managing these functions, you will most definitely be concerned as a business owner or entrepreneur. Thus, we will go through a few strategies to watch out for when you assess a company for acquisition or what you need to think about as you build your own business from scratch.

Accounts Receivable

Management of accounts receivable is a crucial concern to generate cash flow. One of the best ways to stay on top of accounts receivable is to run reports on the "aging" of the invoices. Typically, the aging of customer invoices will show you the open invoices in categories of 30-day increments (Figure 16).

Example Aging of Accounts Receivable					
	Current 1-30	31-60 Days	61-90 Days	91-120 Days	Over 120 Days
ABC Company	$ 4,000.00				
XYZ Company					$ 6,000.00
ZTC Company		$2,000.00			
TOTALS	$ 4,000.00	$2,000.00	$ -	$ -	$ 6,000.00

Figure 16   Example of A/R Aging Report

In the next section that describes ratios, the ratios that relate to accounts receivable are the accounts receivable turnover rate and the days sales outstanding, and the overall cash conversion cycle. Thus, when you are assessing how the company is managing accounts receivable as an element of working capital, those ratios help you determine what is going on and if the cash is being managed efficiently.

Remember, too, accounts receivable, depending on how large a company is, that ONE account line on the balance sheet can actually represent hundreds or thousands of customers. Thus, if you have access to the underlying data, rather than just the 10-k or top-level financial statements, you can also calculate customer groupings or other categories of customers. Remember, that aging report can tell you if the aging is mostly current or trending toward not being current. Sometimes we cannot see the aging of the open accounts receivable or do some of the calculations on categories of customers or by regions of the company or states. There could be issues underneath these year-over-year comparisons, which is why you want to see consistent performance over time.

Inventory

Inventory management is an important thing to pay attention to because of the amount of money that can be tied up in your inventory waiting to be sold. Plus, as mentioned previously, you may have inventory that is not sold, so you want to make sure all inventories are moving as quickly as possible and thus being turned into cash as quickly as possible. If you do have the inventory, you do not sell, and you just want to make sure that the inventory is being used. Regardless of whether inventory is sold or used internally, here are ways to ensure that you are maximizing the cash you have invested in this asset.

Now, inventory can be large bucket money that is invested; however, not all inventory accounts are for resale. Thus, when we examine inventory, breaking out the different kinds of inventory can be very useful. Even if an inventory account is NOT for resale, we want to make sure the inventory is being used and not just tying up our cash flow.

When we examine a company and its financial statements, we will often only see that high-level, consolidated inventory value on the balance sheet. If you are analyzing the company financials of a business you work for, you should obtain a breakdown of the specific types of inventory. Do you have a raw materials inventory? Do you have a finished goods inventory? Do you have a work-in-process inventory? Do you have a maintenance inventory?

If we only have the high-level number for inventory, then we can calculate and evaluate the inventory turnover ratio and days sales in inventory ratios. Suppose we can obtain some detail on the inventory accounts. In that case, we can calculate the second level of analysis on the inventory turnover ratio and the day's sales in inventory ratio. Plus, if you are up to the challenge, you could prepare these calculations for each specific product or product category. The detail of your analysis can go that deep!

Remember, too, that many software packages today have some of these calculations built into them. Thus, if you examine your company or assess a company as an acquisition, you may want to ask about the inventory management systems and see if a report calculates this for you. However, even if that is not available, you know how to calculate this now, and you can ask for information to help you assess this data.

In the next section that describes ratios, the ratios that relate to inventory are the inventory turnover rate and the days sales in inventory, and the overall cash conversion cycle. Thus, when you are assessing how the company is managing inventory as an element of working capital, those ratios help you determine what is going on and if the cash is being managed efficiently.

Accounts Payable

Accounts payable management is all about holding onto cash for as long as possible. Of course, a company can delay the payment; however, it is advised not to do that because it can impact your credit rating over time as a company. But there are legitimate ways to hold onto cash for as long as possible or maximize your suppliers' payments.

One way to do this is to take advantage of discounts offered by your suppliers. Since cash used for paying bills often does not earn large amounts of interest these days, taking advantage of discounts offered by your suppliers could be a better rate of return on your money. Think of it this way, and if your supplier offers you a 2% discount to pay your bill in 15 days, and your bank is only paying you a fraction of a percentage point on your money at the bank, then there is no reason to hold onto the money.

In addition, we, today, can transfer money by electronic means. Thus, we have the luxury of waiting until the last day or two of our credit terms to send money to a supplier. Thus, we can hold money for as long as possible and still get a payment to the supplier within the terms of our credit agreement. That way, if we are earning even a small amount of interest on our money at the bank, then we can hold onto the money to let it keep earning for us.

In the next section that describes ratios, the ratios that relate to accounts payable are the accounts payable turnover rate and the days payables outstanding, and the overall cash conversion cycle. Thus, when you are assessing how the company is managing accounts payable as an element of working capital, those ratios help you determine what is going on and if the cash is being managed efficiently.

Remember, too, accounts payable, depending on how large a company is, that ONE account line on the balance sheet can represent hundreds or thousands of suppliers. Thus, if you have access to the underlying data, rather than just the 10-k or top-level financial statements, then you can also calculate data on customer groupings or other categories of suppliers. Remember, that aging report can tell you if the aging is mostly current or trending toward not being current. We can evaluate the aging overall or do some of the calculations on categories of suppliers or by regions of the company or states, so there could be issues underneath these year-over-year comparisons, which is why you want to see consistent performance over time.

Part Four: What to Watch Out For

- Cash flow statements show you how cash is generated and used in the company.

- Cash can be generated and used through the operations of the business.
- Cash can be generated and used through financing activities.
- Cash can be generated and used through the investing activities of the business.

Part Four: Exercises, Practice, and Resources

Learning activities:

1. Over a five-year time frame, is the company showing solid growth in cash being generated from operations?
2. What is included in the investing section? Is cash usually being used or generated from that section of the cash flow statement?
3. What is included in the financing section? Is cash usually being used or generated from that section of the cash flow statement?
4. It may take a few attempts to understand the changes in the cash flow statement, so find a good accounting resource to help explain it!
5. Always keep in mind working capital management when looking at the operations section. How well is the company managing its working capital (accounts receivable, inventory, and accounts payable)?
6. Most often, you may be comparing year over year. However, you can also compare quarter to quarter, or first quarter to first quarter, or second quarter to second quarter. Different ways of slicing the data can give you specific insights!
7. Now that you have studied all three financial statements, which one do you think gives you the best information about the company? Which do you think gives you the best information about financial performance?
8. At this juncture in your study, which company is performing best? You can include the income statement, balance sheet, and cash flow statement in your assessment overall.

Notes

1 Cash flow statement. Retrieved from https://corporatefinanceinstitute.com/resources/knowledge/accounting/cash-flow-statement%E2%80%8B/

2 Everything you need to know about EBITDA (2021). Retrieved from https://money.usnews.com/investing/investing-101/articles/everything-you-need-to-know-about-ebitda

3 Working capital management. Retrieved from https://corporatefinanceinstitute.com/resources/knowledge/finance/working-capital-management/

4 Working Capital Management (n.d.). Retrieved from the CFA Institute https://www.cfainstitute.org/sitecore/content/CFAI/Home/membership/professional-development/refresher-readings/2020/working-capital-management

PART FIVE
THE POWER OF FINANCIAL RATIOS

Financial ratios can give you quite a bit of insight into a company.[1] The key is to understand what you are looking for and how to interpret the numbers. In this section, several different ratios will be explored using the two companies as a source of information to illustrate the power of these ratios. This knowledge serves two purposes. For one purpose, you can see how this information is gathered and from what sources, and the other purpose is to see how these ratios are applied.

In addition to this, you can then use this as a model for analyzing a company you work for, or you can use this as a model for analysis of a company you are considering purchasing or use this as a model to determine if you want to invest in a specific company. You can also use this as a model by which you study a company that you invest in financially. These ratios can be used in all of these scenarios to help paint a picture of financial performance. Plus, if you look at this data every month, every quarter, or every year, you will gain insight into financial performance, and you will be training your financial intelligence to where the hyperbole of any executive will not sway you. Training your gut to be aware of the information that the results of these ratios give you can prove invaluable.

Within this section of the book, you will be learning about ratios that fall into four distinct categories. These categories are **profitability, solvency, liquidity**, and **activity** ratios.[2] The profitability ratios look at a company's ability to consistently generate or grow its gross margins and net profit margins. You are aware that profit is an estimate, but you know that a business's operations generate and use cash. Thus, even though you could be looking at estimated numbers and know why they are estimated, you can still see how easily cash is being generated and used in the company.

DOI: 10.1201/9781003110613-5   **81**

For the solvency ratios, you are looking at the company's long-term prospects – you will be able to assess if the company maybe exist as a viable company in the foreseeable future. This analysis is an important measure because the calculations include the company's long-term assets and long-term debt.

You will also examine and learn how to use liquidity ratios. These ratios tell you how well the company can pay its bills in the short term. These ratios show you the ability to turn current assets into cash to cover those short-term or immediate debts (liabilities).

The last category of ratios is the activity ratios. These are another way of looking at cash usage and generation of cash and how well you are managing your working capital. You will assess how well a company manages its cash by how well they manage accounts receivable, accounts payable, and inventory.

Finally, you will also do some analysis on free cash flow and how that ties to the earnings before interest, taxes, depreciation, and amortization. It is important to keep it clear in your mind how to handle the non-cash deductions, like depreciation and amortization, and how those are handled when understanding cash flow.

Honestly, commit to analyzing these ratios for a company you work for as a baseline of your learning journey. You will start to see just how powerful these numbers are in understanding financial performance. For instance, sometimes, it can be difficult to determine if bad financial decisions are being made. Still, ratios can often point to the possibility that bad financial decisions are being made.

For example, in 2009, General Motors filed for bankruptcy.[3] If you had been examining the financial statements up to that point, the bankruptcy would not have been surprising to you. You may not have predicted a bankruptcy was going to happen, but you would have seen a financial performance that definitely headed in the wrong direction. Suppose you can read the financial statements and do some quick calculations and do this over a long period of time. In that case, your instincts will tell you something is not right, and then you can assess what you would like to do about the situation as an employee or an investor.

The one thing you want to watch out for is just how similar the business models are to any company you are comparing. No two companies are ever 100% alike. However, in this book, one of our main analyses is comparing LogMeIn to Zoom. The reason for the comparison is that both of these companies offer virtual meeting technology. Any company you want to compare, you can Google which competitors they are most customarily compared to financially. Or you can find sources on Google that tell you the industry code for the company (this can also be in the 10-k), which can give you a better idea of which companies to compare financially.

For our purposes, LogMeIn and Zoom have some similar product lines, so there is some comfort in the comparisons even though they are in different industries. If we were comparing Zoom to Boeing, it would be a lot more difficult for comparison purposes. There might not be a reason you have personally to compare their financial performance to each other.

Topic 16: Profitability Ratios

When examining the profit and loss statement for a company, you want to assess how profitable the company is and how that profitability is trending over time. Thus, profitability ratios are a specific way to assess how well a company uses its assets to generate profits.[4]

Since you now understand that profit is not the same thing as cash, then you are looking for a consistency of earnings over time. For instance, it should feel different if a company is showing consistency and growth in their earnings versus a company with huge variations in their earnings.

The **gross profit margin** is a profitability ratio that assesses gross profit on the profit and loss statement.[5] Here is the gross profit margin formula:

Gross Profit / Revenue

Do not be surprised by terminology. In most cases, revenue is the first item on the profit and loss statement, but this can also be called Gross Sales, Net Sales, Sales, Net Revenue, or Gross Revenue. Plus, Gross Profit could be called Gross Margin. In addition, if you are looking up videos or other web content, you could find that the formula could be given to you as:

$$(\text{Revenue} - \text{Cost of Goods Sold}) / \text{Revenue}$$

Revenue minus cost of goods sold is the same thing as gross profit in the previous formula. In addition, if you use this rendition of the formula, the cost of goods sold can also be called cost of revenue.

Gross Profit Margin

The gross profit margin for Zoom and LogMeIn are examined here. From the 10-k reports, we have the following information for the two companies (all numbers are in thousands per the 10-k) (Figure 17):

Company	Zoom	
Year	Revenue	Gross Profit
YR1 2020	$ 622,658	$ 507,262
YR2 2019	$ 330,517	$ 269,516
Company	LogMeIn	
Year	Revenue	Gross Profit
YR1 2019	$ 1,260,385	$ 936,720
YR2 2018	$ 1,203,992	$ 922,511

Figure 17   LOGM and ZM Revenue and Gross Profit Data

Then we plug these numbers into the gross profit margin formula: Gross Profit/Revenue = Gross Profit Margin. Here are the results of the calculations for both companies (Figure 18):

Year	Gross Profit Margin: Zoom			
YR1 2020	$ 507,262 /	$ 622,658	=	81.5%
YR2 2019	$ 269,516 /	$ 330,517	=	81.5%

Year	Gross Profit Margin: LogMeIn			
YR1 2019	$ 936,720 /	$ 1,260,385	=	74.3%
YR2 2018	$ 922,511 /	$ 1,203,992	=	76.6%

Figure 18   ZM and LOGM Gross Profit Margin Results

We are only examining two years here for illustration purposes. Still, if you are studying your own company you work for or examining buying a business or an investor, you want to calculate many years to establish a trend. Two years is not exactly a trend, but we see in these numbers that both companies have a healthy gross profit. Why do I say that? One way to think about this is that even though the gross profit margin here is shown as a percentage, you can also think of it as how many CENTS per ONE DOLLAR of revenue the company keeps. Thus, Zoom (ZM) keeps 81.5 cents of every dollar, and LogMeIn (LOGM) keeps over 74 cents of every dollar of revenue.

The second reason you will learn is that the technology industry tends to have good gross margins. Defining "good" is equal parts art and science. The science is the calculation itself, but the art is that over time you will get a "feel" for the gross profit margin in the industry you are studying. The more you do these calculations and establish a trend, the more you will see how well your industry or company performs.

Another thing to consider is that no two companies are EXACTLY alike. However, if anything ever looks odd or out of place in any results, one good place to look for insight into the numbers is the 10-k report.

You could see (if there is something odd or out of place in results) classified as an "extraordinary" item or something that only happens irregularly. For example, there could be litigation that is resolved where one party has to pay out a settlement on an income statement, which would be an unusual circumstance (hopefully)! When you see something like this, calculate the ratios with and without this entry. You can see the impact of the extraordinary item and see if performance is still in alignment without that effect.

Net Profit Margin

For the **net profit margin**, you are examining the bottom-line profits.[6] Gross margin examines the product line profitability, and the net income looks at the overall profitability after all other expenses have been accounted for in operations. The formula for net profit margin is:

Net Income / Revenue

Be aware that net income can be called net profit.

The net profit margin for Zoom and LogMeIn are examined here. From the 10-k reports, we have the following information for the two companies (all numbers are in thousands per the 10-k) (Figure 19):

Company	Zoom	
Year	Revenue	Net Profit
YR1 2020	$ 622,658	$ 26,362
YR2 2019	$ 330,517	$ 8,349
Company	LogMeIn	
Year	Revenue	Net Profit
YR1 2019	$ 1,260,385	$ (14,555)
YR2 2018	$ 1,203,992	$ 74,371

Figure 19   LOGM and ZM Revenue and Net Profit Data

Then we plug these numbers into the net profit margin formula: Net Profit/Revenue = Net Profit Margin. Here are the results of the calculations for both companies (Figure 20):

Year	Net Profit Margin: Zoom		
YR1 2020	$ 26,362 / $ 622,658 =	4.2%
YR2 2019	$ 8,349 / $ 330,517 =	2.5%

Year	Net Profit Margin: LogMeIn		
YR1 2019	$ (14,555) / $ 1,260,385 =	-1.2%
YR2 2018	$ 74,371 / $ 1,203,992 =	6.2%

Figure 20   ZM and LOGM Net Profit Margin Results

Just like the gross profit margin, instead of looking at this as a percentage, we can think of it as the CENTS leftover from EACH dollar of revenue after ALL expenses have been recognized. Therefore, for Zoom (ZM), the most recent year sees them keeping four cents of every dollar they generate in revenue.

Now, four cents may not sound like a lot, but remember, Zoom (ZM) generated $622,650,000 in revenue (because the number in the table is THOUSANDS; thus, we have to add three zeros to it to know the full revenue earned). Therefore, the net profit of $26,362 is $26 MILLION.

Connecting Back to the 10-k

As you study the gross profit and net profit margins of a company, keep in mind that you may start having questions about the results. One way to find answers to your questions is to refer back to the 10-k to find possible answers to questions. Thus, in the case of profitability, you can search on various terms to find out more information that might explain certain results you are seeing. You may want to search on terms like revenue, profit, margin, or extraordinary expenses.

As you study different companies and build upon your financial intelligence, you may have other search terms that you decide are important. It is not intended to be an exhaustive list. You can also take these search terms to Google or whichever Internet provider platform you have and search on those terms to see what experts may be saying about the company and their results.

For example, for Zoom and LogMeIn, the gross margins are very healthy and pretty consistent for the two years that we have examined in the book. But the net profit margins for our small sample of data have quite some variation. For Zoom, this may be because they have had a boom in sales, making them more profitable and boosting profitability. But what is happening with LogMeIn? 2019 is showing a net loss, and 2018 showed a net profit. One thing to notice about this is that if you look in the 10-k and look specifically at the income statement on page 55 of the 2019 10-k, you will notice a couple of accounts that are not consistent from year to year. In 2019, there was a restructuring charge. If you search on the word "restructuring," you find a note explaining a reduction in force (think layoffs).[7] So, this is a one-time event and will not be happening every single year.

In addition, LogMeIn in 2018, there was an unusual item on the income statement called a "gain on disposition of assets." If you search on the word "gain," you will find a note on page 70 regarding a divestiture (sale) of a business called Xively.[8] This does not explain all of the differences, but it gives us some insight into some unusual situations each year. The other thing you will want to do is possibly do a horizontal analysis to find the rest of the influences that make the net profitability have so much variation for LogMeIn.

When you do have an unusual item like that, you can calculate the ratios without that number in the calculations when it does not happen every year. You can then see how much the results align from year to year without that unusual item in the totals. Take a look at results compared to the totals having the gain on that disposition in the numbers versus NOT having the gain in the numbers (Figure 21):

Year	Net Profit Margin: LogMeIn	
YR1 2019	$ (14,555) / $ 1,260,385 =	-1.2%
YR2 2018	$ 74,371 / $ 1,203,992 =	6.2%

Year	Net Profit Margin: LogMeIn (W/O)	
YR1 2019	$ (14,555) / $ 1,260,385 =	-1.2%
YR2 2018	$ 40,461 / $ 1,203,992 =	3.4%

Figure 21   LogMeIn Results: Unusual Item

We can see here that the unusual activity of selling a business unit inflated the net profit margin by a bit over 3%.

Topic 17: Solvency Ratios

Solvency is a way of examining a company's balance sheet to get a feel for how the company might exist beyond the short term.[9] The goal, of course, is that the company will continue to operate into the foreseeable future and that the burden of liabilities will not impede those operations. Think of these long-term liabilities as the long-term debt, or financial leverage, of a company.

When you think about financial leverage in a company, you want to examine and assess just how much debt financing, or borrowing, a company is doing in the long term.

Companies can take out long-term loans, mortgage, or issue bonds to the public to invest in that must eventually be paid back to those investors. The financial statement that you want to examine for long-term borrowing and liabilities is the balance sheet.

Debt to Assets

Another financial ratio that can be useful to you is to examine the **debt to assets ratio**[10]. The result will let you know how much debt is financing your assets. Again, preferably, this result should be less than 1, or the smaller, the better.

The formula for the debt to assets ratio is:

Total Debt / Total Assets

Equity to Assets

Another financial ratio that can be useful to you is to examine the **equity to assets ratio**[11]. The result will let you know how much equity is financing your assets. Again, preferably, this result should hopefully be a bigger slice of the pie than debt. The

The formula for the equity to assets ratio is:

Total Equity / Total Assets

Debt to Equity

One ratio you can use to examine solvency is the **debt to equity ratio**[12]. The formula works like this:

Total Liabilities / Total Shareholder Equity

A small result is what you are looking for in terms of financial health.

Zoom Results

Here are selected items from the 10-k for Zoom (ZM) to calculate these solvency ratios (Figure 22):

Year	Zoom		
YR1 2020	Total Assets	$	1,289,845
YR1 2020	Total Liabilities	$	455,902
YR1 2020	Total Equity	$	833,943
YR1 2019	Total Assets	$	354,565
YR1 2019	Total Liabilities	$	202,452
YR1 2019	Total Equity	$	152,113

Figure 22 Zoom Solvency Data

Note here that the 10-k information did not show a correct number for the total equity. The total equity number had left out the amount for convertible preferred stock. The reason the error was caught is because of the accounting equation. The assets have to equal the liabilities plus the equity. When these numbers did not add up, the difference was the amount in the convertible preferred stock account; thus, that number was added back in to arrive at the total equity in 2019 is $152,113 rather than the negative $7,439 that is showing in the 10-k report.

Once we plug in all the numbers, we get the following results for Zoom (ZM) (Figure 23):

Year	Debt to Assets: Zoom			
YR1 2020	$	455,902 / $	1,289,845 =	35.3%
YR2 2019	$	202,452 / $	354,565 =	57.1%
Year	Equity to Assets: Zoom			
YR1 2020	$	833,943 / $	1,289,845 =	64.7%
YR2 2019	$	152,113 / $	354,565 =	42.9%
Year	Debt to Equity: Zoom			
YR1 2020	$	455,902 / $	833,943 =	54.7%
YR2 2019	$	202,452 / $	152,113 =	133.1%

Figure 23   Zoom Solvency Ratios

In 2019, we can see from these numbers, the equity was 42.9% of the total assets and liabilities (debt) was 57.1% of assets. This data, if we think of assets as the total pie, can be split up in terms of equity and liabilities as shown here (Figure 24):

Figure 24   Zoom 2019 Split of Debt and Equity to Assets

For 2019, 42.9% of the assets were financed by equity, and 57.1% were financed by debt (liabilities). Another way to say it is that 42.9% plus the 57.1% = 100% of assets on the balance sheet.

For 2020, debt was reduced, as seen in this graphic (Figure 25):

Figure 25   Zoom 2020 Split of Debt and Equity to Assets

For 2020, the debt was reduced from 57.1% in 2019 to 35.3%. Most companies will carry some debt, but just like with individuals, we do not want to have more debt than equity (think the net worth of an individual).

These results help explain the debt to equity ratio. For example, in 2019, the Zoom debt to equity ratio was 133.1%, meaning that the company had a much larger debt than it did equity, but that turned around significantly in 2020. By 2020, the debt was only about half of the equity, which is a much better position!

LogMeIn Results

Here are selected items from the 10-k for Zoom (ZM) to calculate these solvency ratios (Figure 26):

Year	LogMeIn		
YR1 2019	Total Assets	$	3,855,997
YR1 2019	Total Liabilities	$	1,115,289
YR1 2019	Total Equity	$	2,740,708
YR1 2018	Total Assets	$	3,935,953
YR1 2018	Total Liabilities	$	961,265
YR1 2018	Total Equity	$	2,974,688

Figure 26   LogMeIn Solvency Data

For LogMeIn (LOGM), when the numbers are input into the formulas, we obtain the following results (Figure 27):

Year	Debt to Assets: LogMeIn		
YR1 2019	$ 1,115,289 / $	3,855,997 =	28.9%
YR1 2018	$ 961,265 / $	3,935,953 =	24.4%
Year	Equity to Assets: LogMeIn		
YR1 2019	$ 2,740,708 / $	3,855,997 =	71.1%
YR1 2018	$ 2,974,688 / $	3,935,953 =	75.6%
Year	Debt to Equity: LogMeIn		
YR1 2019	$ 1,115,289 / $	2,740,708 =	40.7%
YR1 2018	$ 961,265 / $	2,974,688 =	32.3%

Figure 27 LogMeIn Solvency Ratios

For LogMeIn, in 2018, 24.4% of assets were financed by debt, and 75.6% of assets were financed by equity. The 24.4% debt to assets ratio plus the 75.6% equity to assets ratio equals 100%. Compared to Zoom. LogMeIn carries less debt than they do; however, the debt as a percentage of equity is on the rise, but it is still lower than Zoom's result.

Connecting Back to the 10-k

First, before referring back to the 10-k for these two companies, think about what high levels of debt feel like in your personal life. For instance, if you keep track of your net worth (i.e., balance sheet) and have $500,000 worth of assets. How would you *feel* if you had $20,000 in long-term debt? How would you *feel* if you had $100,000 in long-term debt? Or how would you feel if you have $450,000 in long-term debt? As the debt increases, your net worth decreases, or as your debt decreases, your net worth increases. When you are locked into servicing large amounts of debt, your choices go down about what you can do with your assets.

Thus, the same situation exists for a company. Carrying larger and larger amounts of long-term debt can cause problems down the road, especially if you encounter economic conditions where you are not generating as much cash as you used to in your operations.

Both of these companies have a good balance between equity (i.e., think net worth) and long-term debt. You generally want to see, as a general guideline, that your debt is a fraction of the total assets. Many companies can last a long time with debt levels at 60%, maybe even 70%, but that is when economic conditions are good. What happens when economic conditions go wrong as they did with COVID-19? A good financial officer will try to keep long-term debt to a minimum. It might even be a good idea to talk with a Chief Financial Officer about how they manage these numbers!

For both LogMeIn and Zoom, if you search through the 10-k's using search terms like "debt" or "financing," you will find a few notes. Many of the notes are in the highlighted risks to the business. Those can be interesting to read through to get a sense of what each business is concerned with when it comes to debt. Amazingly enough, if you search on the term "solvency," neither 10-k report says anything about that! You can always go to the web and look for information about analysts' opinions about these companies and building the ratios for more years backward so that you can see a clear trend. Looking at only two years is a very short window for comparing these numbers.

However, as you do these calculations more and more and build upon your financial intelligence, you will get a "feel" for a company and its performance. For instance, I have worked for Starbucks as an accountant and in information technology groups. Because I also teach this subject, I have used Starbucks financials in many classes to discuss these concepts.

More about Developing a "Gut Feel"

I have studied Starbucks' financial statements for over a decade, and usually, when I calculated debt to assets, Starbucks was around 50-60% for many years. However, in January 2020, I was teaching a graduate class. I calculated the debt to assets ratio, and the result came out to over 100% (which means that the equity went *negative* for the first time since I had been studying the company).

As we discussed the results, we searched in the 10-k and on the web to explain this enormous change in results. What we found was an article by Cannivet (2019) that discussed the financial decisions Starbucks had made to increase their debt to such levels.[13] I stated in the class that IF there were to be a major economic event that would cause Starbucks, a former employer to have a challenge generating sales, this is potentially not a good position to be in and little did we know that the COVID-19 outbreak in the world was coming that March/April. Now, this performance does not in any way indicate that Starbucks was going to go out of business, BUT the decisions could give you a pause.

What Starbucks was doing, as many companies were doing, was going into DEBT to buy back stock and to pay out shareholder dividends. There is an idea in personal investing called "good debt" versus "bad debt."[14] The article examines what these terms may mean, but going into debt to build a manufacturing facility that will directly lead to more sales is what I would classify as good debt. However, to pay dividends or to invest in stock buybacks, those activities do not generally lead to future cash flow, and thus, it did not feel like a great financial decision.

It was useful information for me on whether or not I wanted to continue investing in buying stock in the company. I have bought and sold a lot of Starbucks stock over the years. I change my investing strategy for Starbucks during the COVID-19 period to watch how that situation played out. This analytical approach and connection is the ability you can cultivate in yourself to determine your own choices.

One other note about this "gut feel." In 2007, Starbucks stock was falling like a rock. I remember several internal conversations about the company stock price and leadership. I was not convinced that it was an operational problem. Due to that belief, Starbucks stores shut down in early 2008 for training.[15] At the time, I had a conversation with someone where I stated that I did not believe that the company's operations were "off." I believed there was something else happening. Not too long after that conversation, we found out the economic reality that caused the drop in the stock.

See, buying a cup of coffee is not generally an "essential" purchase for people. Thus, one of Starbucks' metrics to share in their financials each quarter was a "foot traffic" number. Well, this foot traffic metric had been falling. In hindsight, the reason was that people were feeling the tight wallet due to the financial collapse coming in the real estate market. When the financial collapse started to occur, it made sense that foot traffic would have been falling for a little while because a company like Starbucks is likely a leading indicator of what may be happening in the economy. In other words, people were being affected by losing their homes, and when that happens, they focus only on essential purchases.

As you study a company you work for, you will develop this same sense of the truth about financial performance. As you gain confidence in your ability to do this, you will feel very comfortable assessing a company for acquisition if you want to buy a business as an entrepreneur!

Topic 18: Liquidity Ratios

Liquidity ratios are assessing the short-term financial health of an organization. These ratios let you know if the company can pay its bills or obligations in a time frame of a year or less.

Current Ratio

The **current ratio** is a very common ratio for assessing a company's ability to pay short-term debts.[16] This ratio is calculated using the following formula:

Current Assets / Current Liabilities

Once the result is calculated, you are expecting to see a result greater than 1. Anything higher than a result of 1 is very healthy.

Quick Ratio

Another ratio, very similar to the current ratio, is called the **quick ratio**. Another name for this is the acid test ratio. In this ratio, the calculation will be as follows:

(Current Liabilities – Inventory) / Current Liabilities

As you can see, the only difference here is that you are taking OUT the effect of the inventory. For some companies or industries, inventory can sit for a long time. In other words, sometimes, you want to see how inventory impacts your ability to pay bills in the short term.

Zoom Results

Here is a graphic of the data for Zoom from the 10-k to input into the current ratio and the quick ratio (Figure 28):

Year	Zoom	
YR1 2020	Current Assets	$ 1,095,522
YR1 2020	Inventory	$ -
YR1 2020	Current Liabilities	$ 333,830
YR2 2019	Current Assets	$ 276,719
YR2 2019	Inventory	$ -
YR2 2019	Current Liabilities	$ 152,341

Figure 28   Zoom Liquidity Ratio Data Input

One thing to notice here is that Zoom does not carry any inventory. Thus, the results of the current ratio and the quick ratio will be the same. Once we input the data into the current ration formula, we obtain these results (Figure 29):

Zoom		
2020	$1,095,522 / $333,830 =	3.28
2019	$ 276,719 / $152,341 =	1.82

Figure 29   Zoom Current Ratio and Quick Ratio

For Zoom, the results have improved quite a bit. For the year 2019, the quick ratio was good, and the results got even better in 2020. What this shows is that Zoom has plenty of current assets to pay for their current liabilities as they come due. We look for this ratio to be one (1) or better, and for these two years, Zoom exceeds that benchmark.

LogMeIn Results

Here is a graphic of the data for Zoom that was used from the 10-k to input into the current ratio and the quick ratio (Figure 30):

Year	LogMeIn		
YR1 2019	Current Assets	$	327,893
YR1 2019	Inventory	$	-
YR1 2019	Current Liabilities	$	524,666
YR2 2018	Current Assets	$	324,951
YR2 2018	Inventory	$	-
YR2 2018	Current Liabilities	$	622,657

Figure 30   LogMeIn Liquidity Ratio Data Input

LogMeIn also does not carry any inventory. Therefore, their current ratio and quick ratio will have the same results. Once we input the data into the ratio calculation, we see the following results (Figure 31):

LogMeIn			
2019	$ 327,893 / $524,666 =		0.62
2018	$ 324,951 / $622,657 =		0.52

Figure 31   LogMeIn Current and Quick Ratio Results

LogMeIn is not having good results like Zoom. Since the results are less than 1, this means that LogMeIn has more current liabilities that need to be paid than they have current assets.

Connecting Back to the 10-k

As a search term in the 10-k's for LogMeIn and Zoom, inventory does not get any hits (the same is mentioned in the book's activity ratios section) because of the inventory turnover rate and the days sales in inventory calculation.

Since LogMeIn and Zoom create digital products, an insignificant amount of materials are needed to produce the software products. When installing software on a computer from a disc in the early days of software development, companies had to carry installation documents, disc cases, discs, and packaging materials to ship the product worldwide. Today, digital products cost a fraction of those costs and you do not have to sink money in inventory.

Topic 19: Efficiency or Activity Ratios

Efficiency, or activity, ratios are measuring how well a company is managing working capital[17]. A company's working capital means how well a company manages accounts receivable, inventory, and accounts payable. In other words, this is a measure of how a company manages its current assets and current liabilities. A company must ensure they are managing their cash in a way to ensure operations run smoothly.[18]

Inventory Turnover Ratio

The **inventory turnover ratio** will tell you how many *times* a year that inventory turns into cash.[19] One way of calculating inventory turnover is to use the following formula:

Cost of Goods Sold / Inventory

Another formula that you can find is the following:

$$\text{Cost of Goods Sold} / \left(\left(\text{Inventory Current Period} + \text{Inventory Previous Period}\right) / 2\right)$$

Sometimes, if the inventory has a lot of variation in it (extreme movements from one comparative period to another), you may want to smooth out the effect of that variation.

One thing to watch out for: Many companies may NOT have any inventory that they sell. Thus, calculating an inventory turnover rate may be impossible. This situation is not an issue at all. It just means that they do not have inventory and an inventory turnover rate, and you cannot calculate a days in inventory ratio.

Days Sales in Inventory

Once you have calculated the inventory turnover rate, you can then calculate the **days sales in inventory** ratio. This ratio tells you how many *days* it takes to turn inventory into cash.[20] The following formula calculates this ratio:

365 days / Inventory Turnover Rate

Zoom and LogMeIn do not have any inventory, so calculating an inventory turnover ratio and days sales in inventory is impossible.

Accounts Receivable Turnover

The **accounts receivable turnover ratio** will tell you how many times a year accounts receivable is turned into cash[21]. Here is how the accounts receivable turnover rate is calculated:

Revenue / Accounts Receivable

You will need to pull the revenue amount from the profit and loss statement, and you will need the accounts receivable balance from the balance sheet. The equation will look like this:

Revenue / ((accounts receivable current period
      + accounts receivable previous period) / 2)

You may want to use the average of two periods because of large fluctuations in the accounts receivable balance. Here is the data that will be used for the calculation:

For Zoom, we have the following input data for the accounts receivable turnover calculation (Figure 32):

ZOOM	
Revenue	$ 622,658
A/R YR1 2020	$ 120,435
A/R YR2 2019	$ 63,613
A/R Average	$ 92,024

Figure 32   Zoom Input Data for A/R Turnover

For Zoom, you will plug the numbers into the formula (Figure 33):

```
Revenue      / Avg A/R    = A/R Turnover
$  622,658  /  $  92,024  =      6.77
```

Figure 33   Zoom Accounts Receivable Turnover

For Zoom, this number tells us that the company turns their accounts receivable into cash almost seven times a year.

For LogMeIn, we have the following input data for the accounts receivable turnover calculation (Figure 34):

LogMeIn	
Revenue	$ 1,260,385
A/R YR1 2019	$ 107,595
A/R YR2 2018	$ 95,354
A/R Average	$ 101,475

Figure 34   LogMeIn Input Data for A/R Turnover

For LogMeIn, you will plug the numbers into the formula (Figure 35):

```
Revenue      / Avg A/R    = A/R Turnover
$1,260,385  /  $101,475  =     12.42
```

Figure 35   LogMeIn A/R Turnover Calculation

For LogMeIn, this number tells us that the company turns their accounts receivable into cash almost 13 times a year.

One thing to watch out for: When you are possibly looking at this for a small business, you might have a much quicker turn-around. For example, I work with a client that is a technology company. They sell a software product, and 99% of their sales come through credit card sales. Thus, essentially it is a cash business because a credit card sale settles quickly. Thus, the only time delay is however long it takes for the business to obtain access to their money which is likely just in a matter of a few days or less.

Days Sales Outstanding

Using the accounts receivable turnover, you can calculate the **days sales outstanding** by using this formula[22]:

365 days / Accounts Receivable Turnover

Then, we can calculate how many days it takes to turn their receivables into cash by using this calculation (Figure 36):

Days in a year / A/R Turnover = Days Sales Outstanding
365 /   6.77 =   53.94

Figure 36 Zoom Days Sales Outstanding

Thus, it takes almost 2 months, 53.94 days, to turn accounts receivable into cash.

Then, we can calculate how many days it takes to turn their receivables into cash by using this calculation (Figure 37):

Days in a year / A/R Turnover = Days Sales Outstanding
365 /   12.42 =   29.39

Figure 37 LogMeIn Days Sales Outstanding

It takes LogMeIn on 30 days to turn its receivables into cash. In terms of this calculation, Zoom turns their accounts receivable into cash at a *slower* rate than LogMeIn.

Accounts Payable Turnover

The **accounts payable turnover ratio** will tell you how many times in a period that accounts payable uses cash.[23] One of the calculations you may see is the following:

Total Purchases / Accounts Payable

In addition, just like previous activity ratios, you can average accounts payable over two periods (the current period and previous period). In addition, there is no such account called "Total Purchases" on any financial statement. Thus, to come up with that number, you can take Cost of Goods Sold + Inventory Current Period − Inventory from Previous Period without being an employee for the company. In using this approach and using average inventory, you would have the following formula:

$$\left(\begin{array}{l} \text{Cost of Goods Sold} + \text{Inventory Current Period} \\ \quad - \text{Inventory from Previous Period} \end{array} \right) \Big/ \left(\left(\begin{array}{l} \text{Accounts Payable Current Period} \\ + \text{Accounts Payable Previous Period} \end{array} \right) / 2 \right)$$

For Zoom, here is the input data for the A/P turnover calculation (Figure 38):

Zoom	
Cost of Goods Sold	$115,396
A/P YR1 2020	$ 1,596
A/P YR2 2019	$ 4,963
Average A/P	$ 3,280

Figure 38   Zoom Input Data for A/P Turnover

Now, take this information and input the numbers into the formula (Figure 39):

Cost of Goods Sold / Average A/P = A/P Turnover
$ 115,396 / $ 3,280 =   35.19

Figure 39   Zoom A/P Turnover Calculation

This means that Zoom uses cash to pay its bills around 35 times a year.

For LogMeIn, here is the input data for the A/P turnover calculation (Figure 40):

LogMeIn	
Cost of Goods Sold	$323,665
A/P YR1 2019	$ 52,104
A/P YR2 2018	$ 35,447
Average A/P	$ 43,776

Figure 40   LogMeIn Input Data for A/P Turnover

Now, take this information and input the numbers into the formula (Figure 41):

$$\text{Cost of Goods Sold} / \text{Average A/P} = \text{A/P Turnover}$$
$$\$ \quad 323{,}665 / \$ \quad 43{,}776 = \quad 7.39$$

Figure 41 LogMeIn A/P Turnover Calculation

This result means that LogMeIn uses cash to pay its bills around seven times a year.

One thing to note: Some small businesses may not have a typical invoice processing department that handles invoices from suppliers. Many businesses could have credit cards charged for purchasing products or services. Thus, the timing difference may be minimal when someone orders to when the money leaves the business. It becomes important to ask the business questions about how invoices are paid – or at least know the split between invoices charged by credit card or debit card and what is handled by the traditional invoice processing methodology.

Days Payable Outstanding

Once you have the accounts payable turnover, you can calculate the **days payable outstanding**.[24] This information will tell you how many days it takes to use cash for accounts payable.

For Zoom, the A/P turnover is 35.19 times a year. Thus, when you input this information into the days payable outstanding formula, then we get this result (Figure 42):

$$\text{Days in a year} / \text{A/P Turnover} = \text{Days Payable Outstanding}$$
$$365 / \quad 35.19 = \quad 10.37$$

Figure 42 Zoom Days Payables Outstanding

Thus, Zoom uses cash to pay its accounts payable every ten days.

For LogMeIn, the A/P turnover is 7.39 times a year. Thus, when you input this information into the days payable outstanding formula, then we get this result (Figure 43):

Days in a year / A/P Turnover = Days Payable Outstanding
365 /   7.39 =   49.37

Figure 43 LogMeIn Days Payables Outstanding

Thus, it takes LogMeIn almost two months to use cash for its short-term bills.

Cash Conversion Cycle

Once you have calculated the days sales outstanding, days sales in inventory, and days payables outstanding you can then calculate the cash conversion cycle.[25] The **cash conversion cycle** shows the net numbers of days it takes to generate and use cash in the working capital accounts of accounts receivable, inventory, and accounts payable.

The formula will work like this:

+ Days Sales Outstanding

+ Days Sales in Inventory

– Days Payables Outstanding

= Cash Conversion Cycle

For Zoom, the cash conversion cycle is (Figure 44):

Zoom	
Days Sales Outstanding	53.94
Days in Inventory	-
Days Payables Outstanding	(10.37)
Cash Conversion Cycle	43.57

Figure 44 Zoom Cash Conversion Cycle

And for LogMeIn, their cash conversion cycle is (Figure 45):

LogMeIn	
Days Sales Outstanding	29.39
Days in Inventory	-
Days Payables Outstanding	(49.37)
Cash Conversion Cycle	(19.98)

Figure 45 LogMeIn Cash Conversion Cycle

A negative cash conversion cycle is a good thing. What it means is that that cash is USED at a slower pace than generating cash. For Zoom, their cash conversion cycle will need to be assessed as a trend, looking at several years, to see if that is improving or if this is the usual performance.

One thing to note: As described in previous information on this topic, the day's sales in inventory may not exist in a business, or the day's sales outstanding and days payable outstanding may be much smaller. The closer you get to the ZERO days of the cash conversion cycle, the more you can consider the business a cash business in their working capital – even if they are using accrual accounting.

Connecting Back to the 10-k

Inventory, as a search term in 10-k's for both LogMeIn and Zoom does not get any hits. The same is noted in the liquidity section of the book regarding the calculation of the quick ratio.

Ties to Cash Flow and Working Capital Management

The activity ratios and the cash conversion cycle, along with the cash flow statement and working capital management are all tied together. For instance, if you are a technology business and all your sales are on credit cards, you turn sales into cash quickly. Thus, you have access to cash very quickly, and you do not have to have a lot of cash on hand for paying bills in the short term as compared to a technology business where you are dependent on the customer paying their invoices based on credit terms. If you have to wait 30 days for the cash to come in, you still have bills to pay during that period.

The basic essence of working capital management and cash flow means the same thing – how well are you managing money coming in and out of the business? For technology businesses, cash flow models are usually the better models in the business community. Suppose you think about some of the largest and most successful technology companies today, like Amazon, Microsoft, Apple, Google, etc. In that case, they are rewarded on Wall Street largely because of their cash flow abilities.

Remember, a negative cash conversion cycle is a GOOD thing. It means that you are GENERATING cash, bringing money IN......BEFORE you have to pay your creditors (cash going OUT).[26] For Amazon, they do so by using a structure where, yes, they have their warehouses. Still, they also are a marketplace for consumers and businesses where Amazon does not always have to house the products in their warehouses. For example, you could have a product that you sell, and you have your inventory, but you show your products on the Amazon marketplace and source the items from your store. Thus, Amazon is taking advantage of a subscription to this service for companies to be on their platform and they may take a cut of the revenue generated.

The future of technology may bring a lot of innovative ideas about how to make and generate revenue for a lot of different companies, the only restriction is how creative you can be in how you envision using technology as a platform. The key is understanding how your creative idea can generate cash flow very quickly while not paying out cash as quickly. As an industry, this performance has been the success of technology so far and you can learn to create your cash flow driven technology platform.

Topic 20: Other Financial Formulas of Interest

There are two other formulas to introduce, the EBITDA and free cash flow.

EBITDA

EBITDA stands for "Earnings Before Income Tax and Depreciation/Amortization." You will need the income statement and the cash flow statement to figure this out.

First, the "Earnings Before Income Taxes" is what you may see as "Operating Profit" on the income statement.[27] Whatever a company may call it, it is the earnings *BEFORE* the income tax line.

Second, on the cash flow statement, you will be looking for depreciation and amortization amounts. Adding these BACK INTO the profit is because amortization and depreciation are ways of handling capital investments' expenses. Thus these deductions are not actual cash expenditures for the company.

Free Cash Flow

Free cash flow is the cash on hand that a company can use as they desire.[28] This concept equates to individual discretionary funds. For example, a company can use the free cash flow to invest in infrastructure and equipment. The company can invest some of the money into securities with a safe return and quickly turn back into cash if the company needs the money. This concept is the same idea as individuals who can use our discretionary funds by investing in something that is not risky but has a good return. Hence, we have the money for a rainy day or invest it in mutual funds, homes, or other assets.

For example, if you know the stock symbol of any technology company, you can go to finance.yahoo.com, enter the stock symbol in the search bar, click on financials, and then click on the cash flow statement. For example, if we use Amazon, stock symbol AMZN, at the bottom of the cash flow statement, the free cash flow is calculated for you. In 2019, the free cash flow was $21,653,000,000. Sometimes it may be hard to fathom a number as big as that, but remember, these numbers are relative.

For instance, a person might have a few thousand dollars on hand, so a company with billions of dollars on hand could be hard to comprehend. However, one way to normalize this number is to look at how long they could stay in business – the same idea as an individual having an emergency fund.

Thus, when you examine free cash flow – how long would that money last if a company encountered a time of extremely reduced or no sales? COVID-19 was a great example of this type of scenario. Thus, for Amazon, how long could they last with no sales?

We assess this by also pulling the total operating expenses on the profit and loss statement. We can look in the same place in finance. yahoo.com and click on the profit and loss statement. Annually, in 2019, Amazon had operating expenses of $60,213,000,000. Remember back when we talked about the time frames of a profit and loss statement? This number represents the total operating expenses for the entire year. Since we do not have access to the 12 individual reporting periods for Amazon's income statement, then we take this number and divide it by 12 to obtain the average monthly operating expenses.

Thus, doing that calculation, we get a result of $60,213,000,000/12 = $4=5,017,750,000. Remember, operating expenses occur EVEN IF there are no sales. Thus, if we have $21,653,000,000 of cash on hand, and we have $5,017,750,000 in operating expenses every month, then Amazon can only last a little over four months with no sales (calculated by taking $21,653,000,000/$5,017,750,000 = 4.32 months).

Just like an individual with a cushion of a certain amount of dollars as an emergency fund, the same principle applies here, and this exercise can certainly give you a much better picture of free cash flow than just the number itself. The sale is different, but the approach is the same!

NOTE: Calculating the number of months the free cash flow can last is not a formal business ratio analysis. However, it is a way of examining personal finance (i.e., in personal finance, this is a way of assessing how long an emergency fund would last). Thus, since there is no formal ratio found on this topic in the literature, an appropriate terminology could be **times free cash flow** – which means how long can free cash flow last without sales personally speaking, this means how long cash will last without personal income.

Horizontal Analysis

You do not always have to do a **horizontal analysis**. Sometimes, if you run into unusual results, it might be easy to pick out unusual items on a financial statement (like our discussion about LogMeIn's net profit margins). However, we could not see all the issues at play with the variation in net profits from 2018 to 2019. Thus, one of the ways you can analyze these results further is to conduct a horizontal analysis.

Horizontal analysis is something where you are comparing one year to another year for a specific financial account.[29] For instance, you may want to see how much the 2019 revenue increased or decreased compared to 2018. This, to do this comparison for LogMeIn, for the revenue account on the income statement, we start first with calculating the dollar change from the BASE year to the COMPARISON year:

Dollar Change = Comparison year – Base year

For LogMeIn, for the data we have for profitability, 2019 is the most recent year. Thus it is our comparison year. We are comparing 2019 to the base year of 2018. We want to see how much 2019 changed compared to the base year.

Revenue for LogMeIn in 2019 (comparison year) was $1,260,385 and the base year (2018) has a revenue number of $1,203,992. Thus, the dollar change for revenue for LogMeIn, comparing 2019 to 2018, is:

$$\$1,260,385 - \$1,203,992 = \$56,393$$

Then, to calculate the percentage change, we take do the following calculation:

$$\left(\text{Dollar Change}/\text{Base Year}\right)*100$$

Plugging the numbers into the formula, we obtain the following results:

$$\$56,393/1,203,992 = 4.68\%$$

Using this approach, we will take the items in the income statement for LogMeIn. We will do a full horizontal analysis to determine what line items are driving the change and variability in net profits from 2018 to 2019.

Here is the data for the horizontal analysis for the income statement for LogMeIn for the income statement (Figure 46):

LogMeln (LOGM)	2019	2018	Dollar Change	Percentage
Revenue	$1,260,385	$1,203,992	$ 56,393	4.68%
Cost of Goods Sold	$ 323,665	$ 281,481	$ 42,184	14.99%
Gross Profit	$ 936,720	$ 922,511	$ 14,209	1.54%
Operating Expenses				
R&D	$ 160,499	$ 169,409	$ (8,910)	-5.26%
Sales and Marketing	$ 461,078	$ 382,997	$ 78,081	20.39%
General and Admin	$ 144,780	$ 145,453	$ (673)	-0.46%
Restructuring charge	$ 14,468	$ -	$ 14,468	0.00%
Gain on Disposal of Assets	$ -	$ (33,910)	$ 33,910	-100.00%
Amortization	$ 157,569	$ 172,539	$ (14,970)	-8.68%
Total Operating Expenses	$ 938,394	$ 836,488	$ 101,906	12.18%
Income (Loss) from Operations	$ (1,674)	$ 86,023	$ (87,697)	-101.95%
Interest income	$ 1,651	$ 1,671	$ (20)	-1.20%
Interest expenses	$ (8,247)	$ (6,342)	$ (1,905)	30.04%
Other income (expense)	$ (588)	$ (556)	$ (32)	5.76%
Income (Loss) before taxes	$ (8,858)	$ 80,796	$ (89,654)	-110.96%
Income Taxes	$ (5,697)	$ (6,425)	$ 728	-11.33%
Net Income (Loss)	$ (14,555)	$ 74,371	$ (88,926)	-119.57%

Figure 46　LogMeln Horizontal Analysis P&L

A few things jump out here. In 2018, the net profit was $74,371. Thus, we are looking for the accounts that will explain a swing from $74,371 to a negative $14,555 for a total swing of $88,926.

We see that cost of goods sold has increased by 15%, and revenue only increased by about 5%. Thus, the increase in direct costs is contributing to this swing. In the 10-k, if we search on the cost of revenue, we find one section that gives us a definition of how the cost of goods sold is derived, and then another section tells us that this section increased because of the costs of acquired assets.

Another section contributing to this swing is sales and marketing expenses have grown by over 20%. By searching the 10-k regarding using sales and marketing as the search phrase, we find that the company is recognizing a high commission expense because of a new accounting rule. Now, you may have to grab an accountant to dig into the complexities of acquiring assets or what this accounting rule is, but what we are looking for right now is, does this make sense? Even though we may not know all the finer details of this, if you talk to an accountant, you would find out that acquiring new assets can increase the cost of goods sold, and a new accounting rule can impact how expenses are recognized. This topic would require a bit more digging for the questions to be answered. Part of the learning is knowing no book will ever cover all the questions you may want to ask, but you will know your resources on where to find more information!

Part Five: What to Watch Out For

- When using financial ratios to assess a company and their financial performance, be sure to look at several years in a row to establish a trend.
- Profitability ratios examine the gross profit and the net profit of a company.
- Liquidity ratios assess the ability of a company to pay its bills in the short term.
- Solvency ratios assess the long-term leverage and if they heavily finance through debt or equity. This ratio is a good indication of the long-term viability of the company over time.
- Activity ratios help you to assess the ability of the company to manage its working capital.
- The cash conversion cycle helps to assess the timing of how a company generates and uses cash.
- Free cash flow is similar to the emergency fund that an individual builds in his or her personal life.

Part Five: Exercises, Practice, and Resources

Learning activities:

1. Obtain the financial statements or the 10-k, or any other financial notes you can get your hands on for your analysis. Gather a few years' worth of data if you can, perhaps at least five years if you can.
2. Obtain competitor information (if possible) or at least look at a publicly traded competitor. It is important to compare!
3. For each year, calculate:
   a. Profitability ratios
      i. Gross profit margin
      ii. Net profit margin

      iii. What trends are you seeing over time?

b. Solvency ratios

      i. Debt to assets ratio

      ii. Equity to assets ratio

      iii. Debt to equity ratio

      iv. What trends are you seeing over time?

c. Liquidity ratios

      i. Current ratio

      ii. Quick ratio

      iii. What trends are you seeing over time?

d. Activity ratios

      i. Inventory turnover ratio

      ii. Days sales in inventory

      iii. Accounts receivable turnover

      iv. Days sales outstanding

      v. Accounts payable turnover

      vi. Days payables outstanding

      vii. Cash conversion cycle

      viii. What trends are you seeing over time?

e. Calculate the EBITDA, compare the net income to EBITDA. How much money is going to non-cash transactions?

f. Calculate free cash flow, or if publicly traded you can go to finance.yahoo.com and look up your company. Once you enter the company stock symbol in the search, you will see a tab for financial statements, and you will look up the cash flow statement. At the bottom, yahoo has calculated the free cash flow for you!

g. Calculate the times free cash flow numbers to see how long the cash balance would last if there is a economic catastrophe. What is your reaction to this result? How many months would they be able to cover those expenses without revenue and cash flow generation?

h. If you see unusual results or variations/swings in any ratios, can you explain why those variations occurred? Part of the answers may be in the calculations of the horizontal analysis.

4. At this juncture in your study, which company is performing best? You can include the income statement, balance sheet, cash flow statement, horizontal analysis, AND your ratio calculations in your assessment overall.

Notes

1 Financial ratios (2020). Retrieved from https://www.inc.com/encyclopedia/financial-ratios.html

2 Five types of financial ratios for analyzing stocks (2020). Retrieved from https://www.thebalance.com/types-of-financial-ratios-2637034

3 TIMELINE: Key Dates in General Motors' History. Retrieved from https://www.reuters.com/article/us-gm-chronology-sb/timeline-key-dates-in-general-motors-history-idINTRE5500ES20090601

4 Profitability Ratios: Measures of a Company's Earning Power. Retrieved from Corporate Finance Institute at https://corporatefinanceinstitute.com/resources/knowledge/finance/profitability-ratios/

5 What is the gross profit margin (2020). Retrieved from https://www.thebalancesmb.com/what-is-the-gross-profit-margin-393201

6 Net profit margin. Retrieved from https://corporatefinanceinstitute.com/resources/knowledge/finance/net-profit-margin-formula/

7 LogMeIn 2019 10-k. Retrieved from https://www.sec.gov/Archives/edgar/data/1420302/000156459020004769/logm-10k_20191231.htm

8 LogMeIn 2019 10-k. Retrieved from https://www.sec.gov/Archives/edgar/data/1420302/000156459020004769/logm-10k_20191231.htm

9 Solvency. Retrieved from https://corporatefinanceinstitute.com/resources/knowledge/finance/solvency/

10 Debt to assets ratio. Retrieved from https://corporatefinanceinstitute.com/resources/knowledge/finance/debt-to-asset-ratio/

11 Equity ratio. Retrieved from https://corporatefinanceinstitute.com/resources/knowledge/finance/equity-ratio/

12 Debt equity ratio. Retrieved from https://corporatefinanceinstitute.com/resources/knowledge/finance/debt-to-equity-ratio-formula/

13 Cannivet, M. (2019) Starbucks' Big Stock Buybacks Limits Future Upside. Retrieved from https://www.forbes.com/sites/michaelcannivet/2019/08/29/starbucks-big-stock-buyback-limits-future-upside/?sh=12cd8ead7047

14 Alvarez, J. Good debt vs. bad debt: Why what you've been told is probably wrong. Retrieved from https://www.cnbc.com/2020/07/20/good-debt-vs-bad-debt-why-what-youve-been-told-is-probably-wrong.html#:~:text=%22Good%22%20debt%20is%20defined%20as,to%20improve%20your%20financial%20outcome.

15 Raedle, J. (2008). Starbucks to close all U.S. stores for training. Retrieved from https://www.nbcnews.com/id/wbna23351151

16 Current ratio formula. Retrieved from https://corporatefinanceinstitute. com/resources/knowledge/finance/current-ratio-formula/

17 Efficiency ratios. Retrieved from https://corporatefinanceinstitute.com/ resources/knowledge/finance/efficiency-ratios/

18 Working capital management. Retrieved from CFA Institute at https:// www.cfainstitute.org/sitecore/content/CFAI/Home/membership/pro-fessional-development/refresher-readings/2020/working-capital-management

19 Inventory turnover ratio. Retrieved from https://corporatefinanceinsti-tute.com/resources/knowledge/finance/inventory-turnover-ratio/

20 Days sales in inventory. Retrieved from https://corporatefinanceinstitute. com/resources/knowledge/modeling/days-sales-in-inventory/

21 Accounts receivable turnover ratio. Retrieved from https://corporatefi-nanceinstitute.com/resources/knowledge/accounting/accounts-receivable-turnover-ratio/

22 Days sales outstanding. Retrieved from https://corporatefinanceinstitute. com/resources/knowledge/accounting/days-sales-outstanding/

23 Accounts payable turnover ratio. Retrieved from https://corporatefinan-ceinstitute.com/resources/knowledge/accounting/accounts-payable-turnover-ratio/

24 Days payable outstanding. Retrieved from https://www.myaccounting-course.com/financial-ratios/days-payable-outstanding-dpo

25 Cash conversion cycle. Retrieved from https://www.myaccountingcourse. com/financial-ratios/cash-conversion-cycle

26 Four Week MBA (n. d.). Amazon Cash Conversion in a Nutshell. Retrieved from https://fourweekmba.com/cash-conversion-cycle-amazon/

27 EBIT Guide. Retrieved from https://corporatefinanceinstitute.com/ resources/knowledge/finance/ebit/

28 Free cash flow (FCF) formula. Retrieved from https://corporatefinancein-stitute.com/resources/knowledge/valuation/fcf-formula-free-cash-flow/

29 Horizontal analysis. Retrieved from https://corporatefinanceinstitute. com/resources/knowledge/finance/horizontal-analysis/

Part Six

Special Topics

There are a few other topics that are essential to your financial education. Many employees in a company, or entrepreneurs, tend to think about how to protect assets or that these concepts in accounting and finance impact them. In this chapter, you will be exploring some of the common controls that you may or may not be aware of in a company. The goal is to increase your awareness, and if you work in a company with accounting and finance resources, they can help you understand the financial concerns your company can address.

One control area is Excel. Some people are familiar with this tool, and some do not use it much, but financial information can be housed in Excel. How can you ensure that the data and information are protected? How can you ensure that the data has not been compromised or is inaccurate? The Sarbanes Oxley (SOX) legislation of 2003 put into law that Excel must be treated as a financial asset when using it to house any information that could impact your financial statements.

In addition, budgeting and variance analysis may be something you have familiarity with already. Still, if you plan a business, you will need to understand some basic information regarding building budgets. This will include how you calculate variances on this data and how to explain those variances.

All businesses may have to answer using contractor labor versus employee labor, but it is a MUST conversation for a technology company or a technology department. Many companies and departments can have inconsistent or wildly varying work needs over time, and contractors can easily fill these needs. You will want to make sure that you can think through these types of scenarios and build out a decision process for yourself and what the decision means in cash.

DOI: 10.1201/9781003110613-6

Finally, the rest of the book addresses issues in small businesses and things you want to look out for in working with, or assessing, a small business. The concepts covered in that topic are varied. Depending on which lens you are looking at a small business through, any or all ideas could be beneficial – especially as a budding entrepreneur.

Topic 21: Internal Controls

When you examine financial statements through ratio analysis, one of the hardest things to do is to try and identify fraud or if someone is "cooking the books." Ratios will give you an idea of how consistent company financial performance is. However, **internal controls** will be a great way to assess for issues that are potentially hidden in the numbers. The important thing to learn here is not ONLY the internal control technique but how to go about asking questions about the technique as it is used in businesses[1].

Segregation of Duties

The idea behind segregation of duties is that no ONE person is responsible for an entire process in a company[2]. Thus, if you desire to be an entrepreneur, you do not want to have only one person who buys your supplies, receives them into inventory, and pays the supplier.

The same idea for an information technology department is present when you have only one person buying computer spare parts, or any assets, receiving them, paying for them, and counting them. While you may trust someone with these responsibilities, theft in businesses can start to occur when there are few or little control around assets of value (especially with cash and your inventory).

Even in a small business, where you may have very few employees or contractors on-site, you will want to ensure that there are places in processes that touch cash or other assets. This strategy includes multiple eyes are involved to ensure no one is mishandling these assets.

It is important, as well, to have standard operating procedures, even for a small business, where expectations for how the process should work are described and articulates what evidence is required of the process to ensure that the process or procedure is working according to the expectations.

Asset and System Access Controls

Asset controls and system access controls are applied in distinct ways. For example, you might have to supply employees with computers and other peripherals (like a mouse, extra monitors, etc.), and these assets must be tracked. Thus, one of the controls over a computer is that the asset might have an asset tag applied. These asset tags are often glued to the computer with a strong adhesive and are very hard to remove. This way, the information technology department can conduct an inventory of the assets to ensure that the items purchased remain in control of the company.

In addition, assets could be locked away for different reasons. For instance, you might have very expensive replacement parts, or you may have products that you sell that are very expensive. Because of the price tag, you may determine that the items need to have extra protection from theft, and thus they may be locked up in some way, and very few people would have the keys to unlock the items.

Products do not have to be expensive to require lock up for safekeeping. For instance, if you have a retail presence in your business and you give away coupons for free merchandise, those coupons may have value on the street. Thus, to keep employees from stealing them and selling them you may need to keep those under lock and key.

Furthermore, your financial information is something of value to you as a business. Thus, any software systems or Excel files should have password protection on the data. Of course, you can certainly teach your employees financial intelligence – that is encouraged. But your financial information, your bank accounts, your credit debit cards must be protected as much as you can.

Physical Counts of Assets

Your assets must be counted to ensure that your books say your value of the assets is accurate. Plus, it helps you to start assessing if there is any theft of your assets.

In the following section on reconciliations, which is closely related to this topic, you would want to count your cash and count any inventory you have on hand. If you have a large inventory, you may want to rotate your counting of inventory by using a cycle counting strategy.

Cycle Counting

Cycle counting is a strategy that focuses on counting more regularly the subset of inventory that moves the most. You can also think of this in terms of the Pareto principle – that only 20% of your inventory drives 80% of your sales, so you want to count those assets a lot more often[3].

Thus, you would split up your inventory into three categories, A, B, and C. The "A" category would be those items you have identified as high value and high turnover. These items you would likely count every single month at a minimum.

The "B" category could be items that are HIGH value and LIMITED turnover or LOW value with HIGH turnover. These you might decide to count at least four times a year.

Finally, category "C" items are LOW value items and have LOW turnover rates. These you may not count but once a year.

This strategy can be important for a couple of reasons. If you are assessing an acquisition business, as an entrepreneur, you will want to know how inventory is counted and make sure this procedure is documented. If you are doing the inventory turnover calculations, you may want to see this data broken out by these different categories or other product categories.

Another important consideration here is that if you assess a business, you may want to consider hiring an accountant or a certified public accountant (CPA) to conduct an audit of the business' financial controls, inventory practices, and other control documentation.

Reconciliations

Part of a procedure, especially around asset accounts, is to do a reconciliation. For example, assume you build computers for a living in a small business. You will have to consider where you will keep your inventory (the physical location) and how you will store this information financially (the digital record).

A reconciliation matches these two "record" locations to ensure that what is represented electronically and what is reported physically are in alignment, and that differences can be explained. You see this in a lot of different areas in business.

Cash register: If you have a retail store as part of your business, you will most definitely do a cash reconciliation on your cash register.

Inventory: If you carry an inventory of merchandise that you sell or inventory of supplies, you will want to establish reconciliation procedures.

Assets: If you have expensive computer equipment and printers or anything else with a significant value, you will want to keep a log of these items with a tracking number and reconcile a computer list of the items with an actual physical count.

In addition, an important concept here is that anytime you use forms for any process, you will want to have numbered forms. This works like check numbers. Think about reconciling your bank checking account (even though we likely use way fewer checks today) it is easy to reconcile a bank statement because of the check numbers. Plus, a nice safeguard on reconciling a bank statement is when you see a missing check number, you then have a signal to question that issue – especially if you are having someone else pay your bills for you. Even without check numbers, it will be easy to see if a transaction is missing in the books.

When looking at a business to purchase, be sure that you are looking at reconciliations on each asset and liability account. This will tell you if you must be suspicious of the valuations on the balance sheet.

Approval Authority

Another important control is the approval authority. This pertains to WHO in your company has the authority to purchase items, sign checks, and to what level of authority (in terms of dollar value) you will allow them to sign off on for the company's behalf.

For example, if you buy computer parts and have someone who buys the parts for you, will you allow them to make purchases up to $500 without your signature? $1,000? What about $500,000? Some procedures will require that a second signature be obtained for any purchase over a certain amount or MULTIPLE signatures for any purchase over a certain amount.

Procedures and Audits

Ultimately, every single idea here, in this topic rea of internal controls, should be documented into formal procedures. Of course, when you are just starting as a sole proprietor, you may not need formal procedures because you are acutely aware of all the transactions in your business.

However, as you grow and hire other people or utilize contractors, what will you allow them to do? How will they be expected to handle the responsibilities you give them? A great way to formalize those expectations are within formal standard operating procedures.

On top of that, you could then hire a CPA firm on a random basis to audit your procedures. This is what the larger corporations do. That way, you can determine if your employees and contractors follow the rules and if any procedure needs to be adjusted.

The bottom line is this: the more you deal with this upfront, sooner rather than later; you will run LESS risk of having theft or some other type of fraud occur within your company.

Topic 22: Protecting Financial Information in Excel

Financial and accounting software often will not take care of everything that has a financial impact on the business. For instance, you could be working for a large IT business or department and all your assets may not be tracked in financial systems.

It is possible that you could work for a company, or think about acquiring a company, and have financial information in Excel. One of the issues that came out of the Enron Corporation collapse and other financial issues is that Excel information must be protected and safeguarded IF the file contains information that could be a part of the company's financial picture.

In this topic, you will learn ways to protect financial information contained in Excel spreadsheets. This is very important because this is now directed by legislation. Back in 2003, when the SOX legislation was passed in response to the collapse of Enron, Excel controls were included as part of the legislation[4]. You would be amazed at how much financial information can be housed in Excel. For instance, in a technology department, you may manage your computer assets in an Excel spreadsheet. You can do that, but you will want to be sure you understand the risks and how to mitigate those risks. This section will teach you what to look for and how to fix any issues!

The first thing to do is to assemble an inventory of any Excel spreadsheet that could have a material impact on your financial statements if something happens to be inaccurate. For example, if you have an inventory of computers in Excel, if any information in that file was inaccurate by $100, $1,000, or $10,000, how would you feel about that? If there was an issue with the file that had an impact of $100,000? Accountants would call this "materiality." Would it surprise you to know that sometimes a company may not consider $100 to be a material error? Frankly, for some businesses, $50,000 might not be a material amount.

The amount of material impact will depend on the value of the computers or other equipment that you are tracking. If the value is $25,000, then will you be concerned about $100? Will you be concerned about $1,000? These are the kinds of decisions you would have to make with your organization's accounting and finance department.

This situation matters because the value of an inventory can be on the balance sheet as an account in property, plant, and equipment. Thus, if a computer were lost, or stolen, would the amount you have to write off be significant to you? Or, if someone deleted a line out of your inventory in Excel be a concern for you? If it is a concern, then you will have to consider different strategies.

Problem 1: Accessing File Content You have probably experienced having a central place where your team shares files (Microsoft Word,

PowerPoint, and Excel documents). These files can be on a hard drive, or these files can be shared on a cloud service like DropBox or Google and Microsoft cloud drives. Either way, the issue is always the same – what if someone can get into a file and they should not have access to the file and its contents?

There are a couple of ways you may want to handle this in terms of file access. In other words, who can access the contents of an Excel file is one of the first considerations. For Excel, you can set a password that allows a person to see the contents of a file and make changes to the file if the password is known to the individual. If the person does not know the password, you can set it to where the contents cannot be seen or that the contents can be seen but not changed (view-only access). Here is a video resource to help: https://www.youtube.com/watch?v=VJqbCpVD-jU

Now, Excel will change over time as new versions come out. Thus, in the future, to look for resources, just go to Google and search for "how to set a password on an Excel file," and you will find many resources. Plus, if you are within the Excel application, use the F1 key on your keyboard, and you can search with the same information and find multiple resources to help you!

Problem 2: Erasing Content in a Cell   One of the issues with Excel or Google Sheets is that contents (data or formula) in a cell can easily be erased – either on purpose or by accident. Would you be able to detect that this had happened? Most of us may not be confident that we would notice that, so the goal is to minimize this possibility from our files getting data corrupted in this way. But how do we do it?

As you are designing (or redesigning) a spreadsheet, you will want to think about formulas, specifically, and not allowing someone to erase those. The best way to do this is through two complementary strategies.

Strategy One: Have formulas that ONLY have cell references or references to functions. In other words, there should be NO hard-coded numbers in the formulas. Take, for example, the following formula:

$$= SUM(A2:A16)*1.02$$

In this formula, cells from A2 to A16 are added up for a sum and then multiplying it by a rate of a 2% increase. Thus, unless you remember that this hard-coded number exists in this formula, this could turn out to be generating data that has errors over the years. Thus, if this "1.02" represents a 2% increase that you are budgeting for this year ONLY, will you remember to change it next year? Or the year after that?

What you want to do instead is have a tab (or multiple tabs) devoted to INPUT data. Thus, if the "1.02" is a rate entered every year, then you want to have a tab that prompts a user to enter that RATE, something like this:

Enter the current year's budget rate :>>>>> 1.02

Then whatever that cell is that houses this number, 1.02, every formula that NEEDS that rate can reference that ONE cell. So, if you only have one formula that needs it or has a thousand formulas that need it, the formula will look at this cell for the data every time. Then, all you have to remember is this input tab and not trying to inventory a thousand cells that need to be updated.

Strategy Two: Once you have designed, or redesigned, formulas in this way, then you can LOCK the cells so that NO ONE can change, alter, or delete the formulas. Here is a video resource to aid you in how this is done: https://www.youtube.com/watch?v=obB7-mKW2OU

Using this approach, you would ensure that certain tabs have formulas only and no hard-coded information in the formulas. Then you can lock those cells down, or the entire tab can be locked if it is full of formulas. One word of caution is to keep track of your passwords because if you forget, you will have to start this process of Excel worksheet development all over again!

Problem 3: Consistency in Data Entry Another cool feature in Excel is the ability to set up drop-down lists for data entry. This way, if you want a product name always to be entered in a certain way, or you have part numbers and descriptions to be consistent, you can set up the list as a drop-down list to choose from on data entry.

Think of it this way, here is an address:
Route 1 Box 10, Columbia Alabama 35432

Someone as: could enter this address as:

R1Bx10,
R1 Box10
R1 BOX 10

And various other combinations of ways, including misspellings!

Thus, if you want to have consistency in certain data, you can make sure that data is "picked" rather than "entered. Here is a video on how this is done: https://www.youtube.com/watch?v=fq-HmPps_V0

Problem 4: Audit and Informational Tabs In any Excel file, an information tab can be very useful. For example, you could have information about WHY the file has been developed, who developed it, when it was developed, and generally how the file operates. This tab can be the files documentation tab, or it can link to a Microsoft Word file that explains how the file works. This tab may also contain change management information (or you may need to make a separate tab for that).

In a change management tab, you could have a table where every change made in the file is tracked. This approach is a form of version control. If you have a version control process, or if version control is turned on if you are using SharePoint, this tab will track all of the changes that have been made over time.

In Excel spreadsheets that have a fiscal impact, an audit tab can be very helpful to users. If your company uses internal or external auditors, then this tab would be for audit testing. For example, if you indicate that a file has a master tab for input data, an auditor can then use that information to ensure that this rule has not been broken. Thus, this tab could have auditing "tests" listed and keep track of every time the file is tested by an auditor and their results notes or link to test documents.

Problem 5: Embedded Calculation Factors   Another issue that can be found in Excel files is embedded factors that are in calculations. For example, you may have a budget file that assumes a certain income tax rate. Suppose that you assume that any sale has a 5% sales tax applied to the transaction. However, you have just learned that the sales tax rate is going up to 5.5% in a few months. What if that 5% tax rate is embedded in cell calculations? If it is embedded in one calculation, so you know where that calculation is located in the file? However, what if the 5% sales tax rate is a factor that is embedded in ten cell calculations? What if it is in 50 cell calculations? What if it is in 100 embedded calculations? You can see how quickly this becomes a problem!

One of the best ways to deal with this is to develop Excel spreadsheets by using an input, processing, and output modeling methodology. Thus, you would have input parameters, like a tax rate, to be on an input tab. The idea here is that you want a tab of input data where you will once, and only once, enter a tax rate. Then, you can have multiple tabs and multiple formulas that point to that ONE input cell. The point is you do NOT want to have a formula with embedded rates or numbers in them. The best practice is to make formulas always refer to cells that have numbers input into them. Thus, the need for tabs to be designated as input, processing, and output tabs. Here is a resource to refer to about this design approach: https://www.youtube.com/watch?v=qxjPKy_Xv10. Remember, you can have multiple input tabs, multiple processing tabs, and multiple output tabs.

> **Input tabs**: One way to use an input tab is to have a tab for those hard-coded rates. Thus, if you have tax rates, any kind of factors like a growth rate in your spreadsheet, or if you have data that you copy and paste out of reports. For instance, many software packages today allow you have reporting come out as an Excel file with rows of data that can be copied and pasted into an Excel tab. For example, if your company uses SAP or Oracle, you can get reporting out of the system in an Excel or csv format that Excel recognizes. The good thing is that some of these reports,

depending on the size of your organization can have hundreds of not thousands of data lines. You can be grateful that Excel can handle a million or more rows of data in one tab!

Processing tabs: Processing tabs are devoted to the transformation of the data in the data tabs. An example of a processing tab is a tab devoted to a pivot table or multiple pivot tables. As an example, you may have an input tab that has thousands of rows of sales data. You may need to have this data consolidated into a monthly total of sales. A way to do that quickly is by using a pivot table[5].

Another way of using a processing tab is when you have to do a lot of calculations. This approach can also include pivot tables for processing and consolidating information from other tabs in the Excel file.

Output tabs: An output tab should be used for printing purposes. Your output tab may have formulas in it where you are pulling data from other spreadsheet tables. Still, the important distinction is that the information is formatted for formal reporting and printing.

This tab can be a great place to have a "dashboard." For instance, you might have charts that are pointing at data in other tabs. These tabs may have header information suitable for printing.

Closing thoughts: The idea here is that you have a solid strategy for developing spreadsheets that help you to reduce errors and ensure the integrity of the data you are using in financial statements. Many companies with Excel spreadsheets drive journal entries or contain other financial information, and you want to be sure the data is accurate.

You can have many of the input tabs, processing tabs, and output tabs that you want. In some files, you may use one type of tab more than others – it is entirely up to you and the particular situation of the spreadsheet. But if you have a methodology that everyone is taught how to use, then everyone can be on the same page on how to protect company financial information!

Topic 23: Budgeting and Variances

Budgeting and variance analysis are important to any business. You will learn the basics of **budgeting** and **variance analysis** and will likely rely on an accountant or bookkeeper with the details. Still, you should also know what these professionals are doing for you to stay on top of their work and ask good questions!

Budgeting

Budgeting can be simple, and it can be complex. The complexity comes in building your modeling for this important exercise and what information you are trying to track. This task requires us to determine the best way to forecast line items on the profit and loss statement, which is the most common form of budgeting for a small business[6].

In a larger business, there will be MANY different kinds of budgets. The budgeting process would begin with the strategic plan – what are the big goals of the organization? How much does the organization target revenue growth? Generally, a company may look five years forward and budget for the most current or upcoming year. Essentially, many large businesses start with a **master budget** that reflects the organization's overall goals. Then the budgets start cascading down into supporting budgets – like sales budgets, department budgets, expense budgets, capital budgets, and many other types of budgets[7].

The key to budgets is determining HOW to forecast budget line items. There are numerous ways to do this, but a few different approaches will be outlined here to get you started. Your task is to know that learning to budget and doing it well requires practice and attention to detail. Think of budgets as a learning process that teaches you about your business!

As an entrepreneur, budgeting comes down to how you forecast your startup or how you forecast and budget for operations if you acquire a business. Otherwise, as an employee of a company, you may very well be involved at some point in your career, having to develop and monitor budgets for a department or other subgroup within an organization. As an investor, you would not likely look at this in assessing a company's financial performance.

Historical Averages

Suppose we have four years' worth of call data that come into a support center for the information technology department. This data could be data that is pulled from a ticketing system.

One way to get an idea of averages is to look at this by calculating the **historical average** of just the January data each year. Then get an average for the data for just the February months and so on. The reason you may want to do this is to avoid seasonality issues that can mess with averages over a year. Consider the following support center call data (Figure 47):

					Overall Call Data in Support Desk 2014-2017							
2014	Jan-14	Feb-14	Mar-14	Apr-14	May-14	Jun-14	Jul-14	Aug-14	Sep-14	Oct-14	Nov-14	Dec-14
	3023	3102	3116	3233	3536	3734	4002	4169	4287	3200	3066	3029
2015	Jan-15	Feb-15	Mar-15	Apr-15	May-15	Jun-15	Jul-15	Aug-15	Sep-15	Oct-15	Nov-15	Dec-15
	3024	3182	3356	3780	3900	4200	4517	4575	4695	3857	3381	3408
2016	Jan-16	Feb-16	Mar-16	Apr-16	May-16	Jun-16	Jul-16	Aug-16	Sep-16	Oct-16	Nov-16	Dec-16
	3327	3510	3788	4199	4475	4527	4853	5031	5264	4527	4223	3768
2017	Jan-17	Feb-17	Mar-17	Apr-17	May-17	Jun-17	Jul-17	Aug-17	Sep-17	Oct-17	Nov-17	Dec-17
	3723	3896	4031	4094	4707	5256	5426	5706	6137	4857	4812	4517

Figure 47   Call Center Data Forecasting Example

If you are looking at this data and you are desiring to forecast, or budget, what 2018 would look like, we can first examine what would January 2018 look like if we only calculated an average of the January 2014, January 2015, January 2016, and January 2017 data by doing the following calculation (or function) in Excel or on a calculator:

$$(3023 + 3024 + 3327 + 3723) / 4 = 3274 (\text{ROUNDED})$$

Now, take a look at this data if we were to graph the data out year over year (Figure 48):

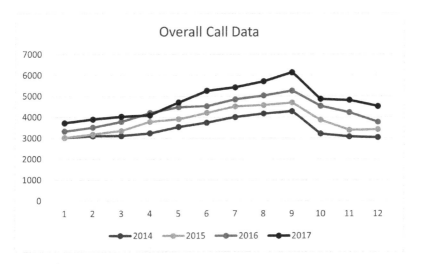

Figure 48   Support Center Data for Forecasting Chart

Here, we can see that each year does follow a bit of a pattern. This helps us a great deal to come up with a budget/forecast. This helps us confirm that doing a monthly average of January, February, March, etc., can be a valid way to forecast the year of 2018.

Another way to approach this might be to calculate the difference between each data point per month, to get an average "increase." For example, for the month of January we have the following data:

Month/Year	Amount	Inc/Dec
January 2014	3023	
January 2015	3024	+1
January 2016	3327	+303
January 2017	3723	+396

Then, if we take the average of the increases or decreases, we have:

$$= (1 + 303 + 396)/3 = 233 (\text{ROUNDED})$$

Finally, our January 2018 forecast would then be:

$$+3723 + 233 = 3956$$

These calculations could be done the same way for the rest of the months of 2014 through 2017.

Trendline Analysis

There are two ways to think about **trendline analysis**. A trendline analysis looks at if there is a pattern that can be seen in the data. Maybe, every year in September, inventory levels increase because you are a retail organization, and you are getting ready for the sales season around the holidays.

You can look at the data for trends from year to year, or you can look at trends from month to month. For instance, let's say that you look at data over a period of months (Figure 49).

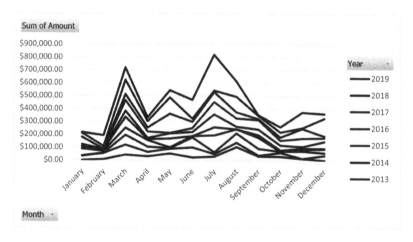

Figure 49   Assessing Patterns in Ten Years of Sales Data

Looking carefully at these months of sales data over several years, you can see a pattern emerge. Sales in March are usually the highest month as well as July and August. This data also shows that each year is generally increasing in sales, following the same pattern.

Cost Drivers

Another way of establishing a budget is to consider cost drivers. A **cost driver** is an activity that drives costs up or down. For example, when hiring employees, there are all kinds of costs in a budget that can be impacted[8].

Thus, a budget line may be directly impacted by the hiring of new people. Thus, a budget line would need input data elements of how many staff currently exist, possible attrition rates if you have a historical perspective of what to expect in turnover, and how much hiring you will do over the budget time frame.

Thus, hiring a new person means that you ADD on a Microsoft 365 subscription, which is an easy expense to forecast based on your expected **headcount** (i.e., number of employees you project to hire.

Variance Analysis When a company budgets (think about this as a forecast for financial activities), you will eventually compare the budget, or forecast, to actual performance. This sequence is how **variances** are calculated; variances are the difference between budgets and actual performance[9].

For example, assume that you have budgeted for travel expenses in a particular month for $20,000 based on a historical average. If the actual costs come in at $28,000, you may have to explain why this line item went over budget by $8,000 (a negative variance). There could be several reasons...maybe the travel costs have gone up. Maybe some extra trips needed to happen because of some sort of emergency that was not anticipated, or maybe more people traveled this month than you had expected.

It is also true that positive variances should also be explained. For instance, if that budget of $20,000 for travel came in as $8,000 actual costs, it is important to explain why there is a $12,000 positive difference. For instance, after COVID-19 occurred, many businesses probably had very positive travel budget line items in terms of planned travel getting curtailed because of an external event that happened to the company.

It is important to determine what is a *material* variance that MUST be explained. Different companies may see different tolerances for variances or different managers for different accounting departments. For some people, anything more than 10% variance one way or the other requires an explanation. For some, they may set tolerances based on dollar figures. The numbers can be surprising.

Would it surprise you to know that I have worked in departments where a $5,000 or less variance does not have to be explained, and I have also worked in an environment where a $250,000 variance or less did not have to be explained.

Why is it important to explain these variances? You want to think of variances as learning opportunities. For instance, you may find that a system or procedure is not working correctly. It allows you to fix a broken process. Or you may find that you need to build the budget in a different way, where you examine some of the cost drivers. For instance, if you have built the budget based on a historical average, MAYBE the budget would be better defined if you determined WHY people may be traveling that month and build a budget around individuals and those assumptions. Over time, as you learn more about the budget, what drives the budget, etc., then the more accurate you can become on predicting expenses and other costs (or even revenue).

In addition, companies are moving to models where they review and adjust budgets sometimes twice a year. Budget assumptions can be way off. For example, during 2020, when COVID-19 impacted the marketplace, a company may have budgets for sales that just did not materialize. Thus, if you kept the same budget without adjusting it, it would not make sense to explain variance when COVID-19 is impacting the numbers so heavily. It does not mean that you do not want to explain the variances; it just means that you want to adjust the budget, so you take out as much of the COVID-19 impact as possible, so you are dealing with other issues in the variances.

The most common budget for a company is a **static budget**. A static budget is usually just one version of a budget based on your best assumptions and models. As COVID-19 showed, a static budget may not be the best approach to budgeting.

Sometimes, a company has various budget versions, such as a worst-case scenario, a likely scenario, and a super best-case scenario. As you get into the production year, you can decide that the year appears to be following either one of the forecasted models and go with that model for the rest of the year. This model is what is called a **flexible budget**[10].

Topic 24: Contractor or Full-Time Employee?

The world of an information technology department is a combination of support services and project-based work. An information technology company will encompass more than that. Still, the concept of outsourcing or hiring contractors to do work versus employees is an important discussion when it comes to information technology departments and companies alike. It is important to develop your approach to making these decisions within your department or company. This section discusses different things to consider as well as suggested approaches in analysis models.

Reasons for Contracting Labor

Many small businesses outsource various activities. For example, consider a legal department. In a large company, having a legal team that you hire onto the payroll could make sense. However, when you start in a small business, you may employ or contract with a law firm to do certain things for you WHEN you need them to be done. For instance, small businesses may need a non-disclosure agreement or some other type of contract. It is much easier and much less expensive to obtain that through a vendor than hiring a full-time legal counsel.

In addition, the same scenario may apply when it comes to services like accounting and bookkeeping or human resources. These are departments you may not hire full-time until you are a large enough business to call for hiring people to the payroll for these functions. Thus, finding part-time contractors can be the way to go before having to hire anyone full-time.

In larger businesses, using contractors can be a solid strategy. For example, from a legal department point of view, you could have a full-time lawyer on your payroll that coordinates all legal activity. However, they may then contract out for legal aid when necessary.

The same strategy can hold for accounting and finance departments as well as technology departments. For example, in accounting departments, the most significant flurry of activities is around month-end. In addition, technology departments have a certain level of support activities they handle for the business, but technology projects can ebb and flow with the business. Thus, it is important to staff yourself for the day-to-day support activities, but when time demands ramp up, you can easily, and sometimes more cheaply, hire contractors to fill out the need.

Another important area for a contractor can be when a specific knowledge base is required. For instance, your company may have grown to the point where you need to implement an enterprise-wide solution to have one database of information on all activities that comprise your sales to cash cycle and your purchase to cash cycle. You decide to purchase Oracle or SAP to process those activities. However, you may not have anyone in your full-time technology professionals who have any experience implementing those systems.

Thus, one primary reason to hire contract professionals is for the specific knowledge they have. You want to utilize these professional contractors to help implement the solution, but you are also hiring them for a knowledge transfer to your full-time staff.

Modeling Analysis

When you have a situation where you do not have the in-house expertise, it is a simple decision to look for contracting help. The challenge then becomes finding the best resource. You can decide to use good interviewing techniques and a good referral community to obtain referrals for the expertise you need.

However, if you are in a situation where you are considering that you neither need to hire a full-time resource, how do you assess whether you directly employ a person to your payroll or if you want to go the contractor-for-hire route? Part of this decision will have to do with the fiscal impact of your decision. Another part of the decision will have to do with the harder to quantify variables. In a large company, you have in-house resources to help you build financial models, either on your team or in the finance or accounting department.

One of the possible reasons you may need this kind of help as an entrepreneur is to build a product or service profitability analysis, build a commission schedule, or build a breakeven analysis, among other possible needs.

Topic 25: Small Business

You can learn much about a company you want to start by working at a company similar to the one you want to open. However, there are a few things to consider in starting a business that are different than the rest of the topics in the book. You can certainly use these resources regardless of starting a business, but most of the time, these approaches will be things that an entrepreneur needs to think about in starting a business.

This section is geared more toward the entrepreneur. This section will discuss various items, at a high level, of what you need to consider as you are starting as an entrepreneur or looking to expand in terms of your business's financial condition and expectations.

Overall Business Resources

As an employee of a technology-oriented company, whether it is publicly traded or not, you would have easy access to accounting and finance professionals. Even as an investor, the accounting, and finance professionals in companies you work for may have years of investing experience; thus, they can be a great resource to you in learning about this specialized area of business and how it applies to your goals.

Thus, if you are reading this book and desiring to strike out on your own in a business, you may not want your current company's accounting and finance staff to know that you want to spread your wings. However, there are resources out there and things to think about in starting an entrepreneurial venture.

The best place to start, especially if you are in the conceptual phase of thinking about starting a business, utilizes the SBA (Small Business Administration). The SBA has many great free resources as a public service to the community – such as webinars, workshops, and probably their most significant SCORE (Service Corps of Retired Executives). Suppose you are just starting to think about putting together a business plan or thinking about buying a business. In that case, these retired executives can teach you about marketing, production, product development, and other areas of a business and the financial considerations you must think about to be successful.

As you start to firm up your plans, you will decide at some point to have assistance from a financial professional. As a small business, you do not necessarily have to hire a full-time accounting or financial professional. Still, you will likely need one or two of these professionals at some point. While there are options out there for financial software, QuickBooks offers a listing of pro advisors. Even if you are not necessarily using QuickBooks for your accounting software, you could find that you need to find an accountant that is familiar with your chosen industry. A QuickBooks pro advisor can serve in that role as a paid professional, while a SCORE mentor is a free resource.

Reports

A few years ago, I interviewed a local entrepreneur for a book on entrepreneurship. As we talked, one of the important things he said to me was that financial information he considered to be an ASSET of his company.

Think about that. It stands to reason that customer files would be an asset of a company, or the vendor files, or his inventory, but HE considered his financial INFORMATION to be an asset. Thus, when it comes to time for him to sell his business to someone else potentially, a person looking to acquire his business would walk into a solid financial information system.

What this means is that the financial information contained in your records is valuable to the company. What this boils down to are the reports and documents. Can financial reports be run for every year, every quarter, or every month? Can information from period to period be explained with backup and proof? Do they even look at reports and know what they mean? When considering buying a business, you may want to watch how financially intelligent the current owner is with the business. Your questions will help you assess this essential element of your assessment.

QuickBooks and Software

When you assess a small business, you will want to be familiar with typical processes in the business that have a monetary impact. Just about everything in a business – business decisions about products, clients, expenses, personnel – all of those decisions flow to the financial statements.

Thus, many businesses may use accounting software, and one of them that is very popular is **QuickBooks**. QuickBooks can be used as a desktop version or an online version. There are other software options out there; however, QuickBooks has a bigger market share, which might provide you a certain amount of comfort in starting a business. QuickBooks (Intuit is the company name, QuickBooks is the product) has pro advisors that you can utilize to identify professionals who are well-versed in the software's abilities for your industry. You can search by industry and other criteria. Here is the link to the Pro Advisors search page: https://quickbooks.intuit.com/find-an-accountant/

One thing to note about QuickBooks is that it is set up perfectly to map accounts to tax items on the 1040 tax form. Thus, once you set up your account and start processing transactions into the software, tax reporting becomes much easier.

However, that is not the end of the kinds of decisions you might want to make on how you set up your books. For instance, the software comes preloaded with a revenue account that represents all of your sales. Suppose you want to report on different sales categories or examine the profitability of different products and services. In that case, you will need more setup in your books. This situation could be a reason why you hire a professional.

QuickBooks has various ways to track information about your business, but you may need a professional to help you figure out the best way to do extra tracking. For instance, you can set up a

PRODUCT revenue account and a SERVICE revenue account. If you have multiple products and services, you can set up different product or service identifiers that map to different accounts.

Plus, QuickBooks features other features that allow you to track project revenue and expenses or classify transactions into CLASSES or by TAGS. Then your accountant can build reporting that breaks out the different classes or tags or projects so that you can see if your products and services are earning adequate gross profits or margins. Not every business needs this level of detail, but it would be good to move in this direction if you have multiple products and services.

In addition to classifying transactions appropriately, this also applies to **direct** and **indirect costs** of manufacturing and delivering your products and services. Direct costs are those costs that can be traced directly to your product or service. For example, suppose you are an information technology services company. For instance, you may provide consultants to companies as project managers in information technology departments. Thus, if you have a client, and they are paying you $5,000 a week for a project manager to run a project, then you know that the project manager you are supplying to that project is a direct cost of servicing that client.

Therefore, if the project manager you supply to the client is paid $3,000 a week, you can add this cost to the project or classify the transaction with the appropriate class or tag to see these costs and revenue together to assess this profitability client.

Indirect costs are the costs we know to go to servicing clients or manufacturing products, but it is harder to trace these costs directly to the client or product. For example, a consultant may service more than one client. Suppose you have two clients that ONE consultant is supporting in project management. Now, the direct HOURS spent on a client is easily tracked by the timesheet of a consultant. However, would you allocate the benefits of the employee against these two clients?

An **allocation** is a methodology that a company uses to split indirect costs by hours, production units, or other cost drivers. For example, back to the idea that the MORE people we hire, the higher a cost moves, we can then evaluate certain costs on activity or volume levels and costs. Thus, if we expected that we would HIRE ten people but only hired eight, that impacts the costs of a budget line item just as much as the cost going up for the line item in general.

Financial Data Analysis

When you are building reporting in QuickBooks (and this can be a similar approach by other software companies like Xero) you want to be aware of "extra" fields or tools that can help you dive deeper into your financial data. Within QuickBooks, there are a few tools that can help you with being able to analyze financial data in different buckets.

For example, when speaking of buckets, we are essentially "categories" of data. For instance, transactions can be looked at by sequence, or by date, through the bank transaction detail in QuickBooks, or you can look at transactions by vendor or by customer. There are other ways to classify data into other types of categories.

One of the ways to classify transactional information is by using a CLASS within QuickBooks. For example, one way this could be used is geographic location or as a store identifier. See, many times, businesses will get this level of detail by creating many more general ledger accounts. With QuickBooks and other software, you may have limits on the number of general ledger accounts depending on your subscription level with the software. A QuickBooks accountant can assist in understanding these nuances and helping you to develop a strategy[11].

Think about using things like classes as a way of analyzing financial data in your business. All of these tools available can give you reporting that enables you to dig into customers or other data pieces to understand your business to a level where you can make actionable decisions.

For instance, assume that you are starting a business doing technical support to small businesses. Some of your clients may use your services hourly, and other clients may pay you a fixed amount each month for your services. In addition, you may have individuals working with you that service these clients when they have issues or need new technology platforms installed.

How will you know if each client is profitable? How will you know if you are chagrining service fees appropriately to ensure profitability? The way that you know is to identify the client on your payroll records or contractor pay records. That way, every month, you can take your revenue and cost of goods sold and break it out by the customer. This analysis is what I call a "margin analysis" report. Here is a sample of what this could look like (Figure 50):

Gross Margin Analysis Report

	Customer 1	Customer 2	Customer 3	Customer 4	Totals
Revenue	$ 3,000.00	$ 1,500.00	$ 1,247.35	$ 2,732.97	$8,480.32
Cost of Goods Sold	$ 1,450.00	$ 1,000.00	$ 500.00	$ 1,600.00	$4,550.00
Gross Margin	$ 1,550.00	$ 500.00	$ 747.35	$ 1,132.97	$3,930.32
Gross Margin %	52%	33%	60%	41%	46%

Figure 50   Sample Gross Margin Analysis

This report can be very informative to the business. For example, maybe this business owner is targeting a 50% gross margin on all customers. Overall, the business owner is not too far off from that goal. Customer 3 has a very nice gross margin of 60%. Thus, it is expected the business owner would then be thinking: Why are we achieving 60% with that customer? Can that performance be replicated with the other customers? The answer will depend – the types of product support could drive the performance achieved on customer three (3) they receive from your business, or you might be using cheaper labor to support that business.

On top of that, what is happening with customer 2? Why is the gross margin so far off from the target? The answer might lie in the labor supporting the client, but it could also be that the client had more problems during this reporting period that required some extra effort to support them during the month.

This analysis is similar to variance analysis. Because you have target goals of gross margin percentages, if you set up the books correctly, you can dive into the data to discover where you can tweak your services and support to achieve your desired financial goals.

This information is how financial data can assist you as a business owner to ensure the viability of your business.

Pricing Products and Services

If you study an existing business, the pricing of products and services should have already been done. However, when assessing an existing business, dig into questions about how products and services are priced. Ask the current business owner how they arrived at pricing and ask them about what specifically are included in the costs of producing the products and services.

It will be important to identify appropriate costs of a product or service to establish solid pricing. For instance, if you are starting a technology consulting company where you provide information technology project managers to companies that need this expertise on their teams.

One of your first questions will be how much would you be paying a consultant by the hour? One great way to establish this number is to look at job postings online for project managers and look for salary information on those job postings or at a website like glassdoor.com.

For example, suppose you find that, on average, a project manager in your area makes $90,000 a year in base salary. If you want to get at an hourly rate, you will take that number and divide by, say 2,000 hours (which is 50 weeks of the year, working 40 hours per week), and you will arrive at $45 per hour. The 2,000 hours assume that the person would be working except for two weeks out of the year (the allowed vacation time you may build into your model).

However, there are other costs to consider when determining your pricing to your customer. For instance, do you pay for any benefits for the consultants on your staff? Since your labor force is the direct cost of servicing a client, you may also want to include health insurance costs. Arguments can be made one way or the other on what you include, but for the sake of argument, consider if you are paying $1,500 a month for health insurance for the employee.

If you take the $1,500 times 12 months in a year, then the total cost for that one employee is $18,000. If you then divide that by the expected workload of 2,000 hours of billable time, you have an additional $9 per hour of costs. Thus, add the $45 per hour to the $9 for a total cost of the consultant being $54.

As you can see, adding on benefits to the resource can increase the costs you are attempting to cover in the rates that you charge to the client that needs project management services. So, what does that mean? Think of it this way…suppose that you are going to charge the client $100 an hour. That seems reasonable, but we need to examine that a little further.

For example, if you bill your client $100 per hour, for the consultant that costs you $54 per hour, you make a $46 gross profit (we arrive at that by taking $100 minus $54). This represents a 46% gross profit (that result is arrived at by taking $46 divided by $100).

How does that sound to you? For some reading this book, your honest answer may be, "I have no idea." That is fair. You want to start with what is a typical amount of gross profit for technology-based consulting services? One source, Macrotrends, says that it is around 40%[12]. Other sources might say something different, but this is a good way to try and validate your rates.

However, if you add any more direct costs for the consultants, you start eating into that gross margin. Another way to look at this is to determine how many hours you think your one consultant will work in any given year. If you assume, they will work a full 50 weeks, then the total gross margin for that consultant to your business is 2000 hours times $46 equals $92,000. Now you can evaluate that amount of gross profit and think about will this amount cover your operating expenses? Will this cover any rent you are paying? Will this cover a salary that you will want to pay yourself? If this amount is falling short, what will you do to make the model work? Add on more consultants to contribute to the gross margin or try to trim operating costs? Or will you work to increase your hourly rate charged to your clients?

Another way of thinking about this is to think about the rate per hour you are charging your client and then compare that to others costs to service that client. For instance, say that you are charging a client $80 an hour to provide technical support. Would that be enough to have good gross margins?

Suppose that you have a resource that is supporting that client that is paid $50 per hour. Just based on the labor payroll cost alone, that is a gross margin of only $30 per hour, or 37.5% ($30 divided by $80). This does not include employer-related payroll taxes nor benefits. In addition, suppose you are assisting the client in obtaining Microsoft Office subscriptions – do you include that in the cost, or is that a separate, reimbursable amount charged to the client? Plus, can you support that client virtually? Or do you have to go to their office and pay for any mileage reimbursement for the associate supporting the client at their site?

As you think through a typical day in the life of client support, you will be thinking of the resources and support you are giving your associates and the related costs of that support. If you do not think about it upfront, you can price yourself right out of the market.

Business Plans

Business plans are not always needed to start a business. So many businesses start as a side hustle, as a side gig to make a little extra income. However, at some point, you may have any number of reasons you want to grow your business or make it a more formal venture. Business plans can serve two purposes: 1) to vet out your idea so that it makes sense to you, and 2) to obtain funding from investors or other sources. A **business plan** is a document that lays out all of the plans for your business[13].

The key is a combination of the type of idea you have and your business evolution. For example, many businesses start as a hobby – like building computers in your garage. You think it is fun, and you do it for friends and family, and then you realize, well, you could do this on the side and make a little bit of extra cash. Or maybe you like to do computer repair, and you will offer those services to people because you are getting a lot of referrals from your family and friends. Or perhaps you would like to support small businesses in their technology needs since many small businesses cannot hire a full-time technology person to their staff.

When you start this way, you may not form a formal business structure, and you would report your revenue and expenses on the

Schedule C of the 1040 tax form every year because you are considered a sole proprietor. A **sole proprietor** is the simplest and easiest form of a business to create[14]. You are so small that you do not need any capital from a bank loan or anything. You just do it on the side when you have the cash to buy parts. Thus, no urgent need to have a business plan since business plans serve the purpose of helping you get funding.

Maybe you perform this little side gig or hobby for a few years, and you do not perform any formal advertising, but your small little business steadily gains clients from referrals. One day you realize, hey, this business could work. Clients are happy, I am providing good value to my clients, so I think it is time to become much more formal in my business. You then decide to place a more formal structure on your business, start a web presence, and advertise.

At this juncture, you may want to take on a different legal structure, such as becoming a **limited liability corporation** (LLC) to limit your exposure to liability as you decide to grow the business[15]. As you decide to grow, you may need to invest in a larger amount of inventory, and you do not have the cash on hand to make a large investment. Thus, you may want to find investment capital through friends, family, or go to a funding source like a bank. When you do that, you will need to have a business plan to talk an investor or creditor through your business model, how you make money, etc.

Now, even though you may not need investment capital, preparing a business plan has merit, even if it will not be shared with others. A business plan allows you to think through the pricing and costs of your business and gives you an idea of how profitable you could be with the business model you are choosing to employ. Going through the exercise can help you determine if you need any capital, when you may want to hire others, etc.

There are many resources on the web for business planning templates and what you may want to include in a business plan for any type of business. As a technology-driven business, you could start with the Small Business Administration and its SCORE (Service Core of Retired Executives) volunteers. They may have a resource that is very familiar with your business model!

Business versus Personal

One of the most important things in building a business is to have a separate business banking account (savings and checking). Keeping your personal expenses out of the business is extremely important and having separate bank accounts helps keep the lines clean.

Now, this does not mean you cannot take money out of your small business. You can. But it does mean that if you are paying your cable bill or paying for other personal expenses, you are doing so with your personal money. You may take a draw from your business or a salary from your business, but then that money goes into your personal checking account and you can pay for any personal expenses you want to from that account.

Receipts and Documentation

Another important thing to examine in examining a business to purchase is to see what kind of documentation backs up transactions on the financial statements. For instance, if you are looking at a particular expense, can you find invoices or receipts for the transactions? It is important to trace that documentation. NOT 100% of the transactions will likely be documented, but you want to see a clear pattern of information and documentation being saved to back up the financial statements. Some of this may be digital or in paper form, and either way is fine.

At the same time, should you do all of the work? Maybe not. You can hire an accountant to help you assess all of these and to see just how well everything is documented. For instance, here are some things that you, or an accountant you hire, should be examining when it comes to documentation:

1. Check to see if receipts or copies of invoices are attached to transactions in the financial software (i.e., QuickBooks)
2. Do all of the vendors have invoice copies on their transactions? These can be digital copies OR paper copies in a filing cabinet.

3. Do all vendors have complete vendor records, including W-9 forms, to identify 1099 vendors for reporting to the IRS easily? These forms could be in digital format and attached to vendor records in QuickBooks.
4. Does the company have inventory? If yes, does the company have an inventory counting policy?
5. Does the company have bank statement reconciliations available, either digitally or in paper form?
6. If the company has a retail presence, what are the company's policies on managing the cash register?
7. Have all tax payments been made on time – you can see this in QuickBooks in the payroll section or in the vendor section (or a combination of looking in both places).

Taxes

Every company will have various demands in taxes at the local, state, and government levels. For an existing company, there will be accounts in the income statement that correspond to these items. Still, an entrepreneur has to be familiar with the particular demands of your business.

Thus, you will need to explore the taxing authorities in starting a business or buying a business. This situation can also be a perfect reason why you hire a bookkeeper/accountant for their expertise in this area.

To consider here, if you have chosen a LLC legal structure, you can ALSO elect to be treated by the Internal Revenue Service (IRS) as an S-Corporation[16]. This treatment is currently advantageous to you in terms of saving money on Social Security and Medicare taxes.

Social Security and Medicare   For example, assume that your business has a net income in any given year of $50,000. As an LLC, this net income would "pass-through" to you and your partners as business income when you file taxes. Thus, you would be paying Social Security and Medicare taxes on that amount. However, IF you decide to elect the S-Corporation treatment with the IRS, you might pay yourself a salary of $30,000. Then the $50,000 that would normally pass through to you would drop down to $20,000, but since you are already taxed, through payroll, for a salary, the IRS will NOT tax additionally the $20,000 that is passed through to your tax filing. Thus, you will save the Social Security and Medicare taxes on the $20,000.

Now, that may not sound like a lot, but what if your net income after salary deductions was $100,000 or even $1,000,000? You can see how quickly the savings add up! Because, a business is responsible for the full Social Security and Medicare taxes, which together add up to 15.3% (that is 6.2% for employee Social Security tax, + 6.2% employer Social Security tax, + 1.45% employee Medicare tax, + 1.45% employer Medicare tax). Thus, if you multiple $20,000 times 15.3%, you are saving $3,060. This result is why you will find that LLCs will elect to go the route of electing the S Corporation treatment with the IRS, and all you need to file to obtain this election is IRS form 2553.

Now, remember, too, if you are building a financial model to model out what this can do for you in terms of tax savings, there is a limit to these taxes and you will want to factor that into your model. For example, the IRS will publish the base salary limits for Social Security taxes on any given tax year. For example, in 2021, this base salary limit is $142,800[17]. This means that if your salary/income goes BEYOND $142,800, you will not be taxed on any amounts over that base salary for Social Security. There is also an additional Medicare tax on any salary that goes beyond $200,000. When you build out this model, you want to build into it all of these nuances to have a solid idea of how you are saving money using these elections.

Consider the following scenario: You are a small business. You have been operating as a sole proprietor and just taking out money and using it personally when you need it. This payment is what is called a **draw**, rather than paying yourself a salary through payroll[18]. Your business has generated a net profit at approximately $20K to $30K a year. We will split the difference here and assume your business will clear a net profit of $25,000. We will also be assuming that your business net profits added to your regular earnings from other jobs will still be under the maximum social security salary level of $142,800 (2021 rates). Thus, your total income is UNDER that amount.

The IRS will assess the FULL EMPLOYEE and FULL EMPLOYER tax on your net profits as a sole proprietor. Thus, you will have to pay the IRS on your 1040 the following amounts:

Employee Social Security	6.2%
Employer Social Security	6.2%
Employee Medicare	1.45%
Employer Medicare	1.45%
Total	15.3%[19]

If your salary from a job, or multiple jobs, is $50,000 and we add the net income of $25,000 to that, then the IRS is looking for social security and Medicare taxes to be assessed on a total of a $75,000 salary. In your job, a payroll check will deduct these amounts, but if you are a sole proprietor that does not use payroll, then your tax bill on 1040 will assess 15.3% on the $25,000 earnings for a tax bill of $3,825 (without taking any other factors into account).

However, if you set yourself up as an LLC, and you set up payroll, you pay yourself a modest salary of $20,000 for the year AND you still net $25,000 that passes through to your 1040 income. You will be assessed the social security and Medicare taxes on the salary you pay yourself, BUT the pass-through income will NOT be assessed the extra taxes. The key for the IRS is that you are paying yourself something reasonable for your business. When you first start your business, the salary will be based on what you can pay yourself, and as you grow, you want your salary to eventually match what a professional would be paid on the market of your profession.

Payroll Taxes Payroll taxes can be handled through a monthly subscription through QuickBooks, but there are other ways to handle payroll as well. As an entrepreneur, if you work through a QuickBooks Online Accountant, at least when this book is published, if you create a NEW subscription through the Accountant version, you can get a possible discount on the cost of the subscription for the life of your subscription. That can be substantial savings.

Even so, some entrepreneurs may look at payroll being handled by QuickBooks and think, well, maybe I can do it cheaper on my own. Processing payroll manually is a lot of time you would have to consider and make sure all of the different payments are made on time. At least through QuickBooks or a similar service, much of the process can be automated, which will save you money in the long run. Learning how to leverage your time is the key to entrepreneurship!

Other Tax Demands   Other taxes can also apply to your business. You may need to pay sales taxes, excise taxes, and licensing fees. For example, in some states, there is no income tax – however, state and local governments may have sales taxes or other types of taxes that need to be paid. Thus, having good records on these taxes and paying them is an important part of assessing a business for acquisition.

Financial Human Resources

Many small business owners do not know what financial resources they may need – in terms of financial advisors and contractors. Depending on where you are in the business will determine the types of individuals you may need to tap to help you.

In the world of finance and accounting, you may need a CPA, a bookkeeper or managerial accountant, a chief financial officer (CFO), or a personal finance advisor (or wealth manager). Wow, that is a lot of people, so how do you know which one you need and when?

Bookkeeper/Accountant   A bookkeeper or accountant will often be the person that is involved in your business the most. They can combine any number of tasks for you, such as processing transactions, bank reconciliations, bill clients, pay bills, pay taxes, run payroll, prepare reports, and do other kinds of analysis for you on the business. Some bookkeepers may just want to process transactions for you, but sometimes you need an operational partner. Someone who can know your business, help you examine profitability, make sure products and services are profitable, etc. So, be clear on the expectations of what you need. Typically, a CPA will prefer NOT keeping your books for you – they may even have a referral they can make to a good bookkeeper.

CPA   A CPA is your tax strategy specialist – helping you not only with the overall business tax liabilities you may have but also in terms of your overall personal tax strategy. Depending on the size of your business, you may want to meet with them a couple of times a year or at least quarterly[20].

CFO   A CFO for hire comes in handy as you grow and expand. A CFO would work with your accountant if you were looking to expand by acquiring other businesses[21]. Or a CFO is a great resource if you are thinking about selling your business.

Personal Finance/Wealth Advisor   A personal wealth advisor may be another individual you want to engage, especially when selling your business. When you are selling your business, you could be receiving a windfall of cash and that might be overwhelming if you have not had that much cash before in your personal life.

Bank Reconciliations

If you are examining a business as your initial entry into becoming an entrepreneur or deciding to examine a business as an acquisition, expand. As you enter into this assessment, one of the things you are doing is to assess financial statements. Still, your examination of the business may need to go further than that exercise.

While it is important to get a sense of the financial statements, you also want to make sure sound business practices have been occurring around the financial information. One of these important tasks are bank reconciliations.

Why is this important? It is a critical piece of information that lets you know that the company pays attention to the financial information. If you cannot get your hands on the last years' worth, or two years' worth, of bank statement reconciliations, then how can you trust the information in the financial statements? A bank statement reconciliation shows the bank balances and all of the deposits and payments, and there should be nothing outstanding that does not get cleared by the next period. It is a possible red flag if the reconciliations have not been completed.

Contractor Payments

Contractors are paid through a separate process than payroll. There is a payment of contractors at least within QuickBooks (other software may work a little differently). Thus, when you pay contractors. You are paying them a total amount of money, and the contractor is responsible for the taxes.

You want to make sure that you obtain a W-9 form from each person or company for contractors. A fillable W-9 can easily be obtained by googling "IRS fillable form W-9," and you can obtain a link to the PDF document. Send that to your contractor for them to fill out, and then you can update the vendor record with the W-9 and attach the form to the record. Within QuickBooks, you also can send a link to the contractor to have them fill out all of the information in the online form. The contractor can also set up their payment details if you are paying them by direct deposit.

In January of every year, your business would then need to file 1099s. The IRS sometimes has two different types of 1099 forms, sometimes just one form. However, if you are using a software system like QuickBooks, they will remind you of these important elements! Right now, you have two 1099 form options. One is for "non-employee compensation," or the 1099 NEC. The other form is for other types of specific payments, like royalties, and the form is called 1099 MISC[22].

As an entrepreneur, if you are looking to acquire a business for expansion or just starting, you want to review if 1099s are up to date and that all of the documentation is secured. Ensure all of the W-9's for all vendors are available and that you can access them either through a documentation system in the accounting software vendor section.

Funding

Not every business will need funding. However, you may need funding upfront for developing a product or need working capital. It will depend on the business idea, your connections to resources, and how the business model will work. Entrepreneurs can get started by generating cash to continue building the business as they go, so you may not need a funding source. But when you do, what should you think about in planning for the funding request? What are funding sources looking for when they review your business and financial information?

Clarity of the Business Model   One area that will be on lenders' minds is how well you can communicate your business model. In terms of the market, industry, products, and services you will offer, how this translates into the business's cash flow and money management. The lender will want to see that you know how the product is manufactured or assembled, what it costs to produce the product, and any other economic risks you face in the industry.

If you are providing a service, the key elements to review with lenders how you duplicate YOU. Often, as a business owner providing a service it is a reflection of your personality and approach. Thus, how you hire will be important and ensure that your customer service approach will be replicated with new employees.

Importance will be placed on building your financial models and budgets, including ensuring that you forecast your sales, purchases, and document your assumptions on how your cash flow will work. Now, this might be easier to do because you may have been in business for a little while and already have a very solid idea of how the business model will work. You can have a pretty good track record of sales and sales growth and then flow the numbers through to the business's profit and loss and balance sheet. It is an Excel modeling exercise and will require a good deal of documentation on your assumptions.

It might be a good idea to go into the business as you start, with financial projections so that you can assess how well you can forecast and budget. If you can do it well, with small variances over time, then your confidence level should be very high that you know what you are doing. If you have to obtain funding before you start your operations, it could be harder to make good assumptions initially. As a result, people often start their businesses as home-based businesses to work out the business challenges as you go, and then when you need funding, you are in a much better position to know exactly what you need.

This will be an appropriate time to obtain a good Excel resource and a good financial resource to build these financial projections. Your job is to be clear on how many products you anticipate you can sell, or how many clients you can obtain in what periods of time, know how many resources are needed to support the production of products and services, and the costs of any materials.

Do the Numbers Make Sense? The financial statements that you are presenting will have to make sense. So, what does this mean? As a lender is reading the verbiage of the business and they start to look at the financial projections or past financial statements, they will be looking at a few things.

First, does the business have the cost of goods sold represented on the income statement? Any time you produce or assemble products OR even if you are providing services, direct expenses exist because of the revenue or sale. If you sell computers, there are component parts that went into building that computer. Suppose you are servicing clients with technology services. In that case, it takes a certain amount of client service from your technicians, or your technology infrastructure may need to be recognized as costs of goods sold or cost of revenue.

For instance, one time I had a client come to me that ran into this issue. They were a construction company, and they had over $3M in revenue but practically no cost of goods sold. It stands to reason that a construction company would have labor in the field, they would have materials they are using in the field, so it did not make any sense that they had over a 90% gross margin. A lender will notice that immediately and have instant reservations about lending money.

Second, do the accounts on the financial statements make sense? One of the things a lender will look at on ANY financial statement is that the account names are appropriate. For instance, does the tax accounts say "Tax Expenses" or "Tax Liability." If the account says "Tax Liability," then the account must be on the balance sheet. If the account name is "Tax Expenses," then the account must be on the income statement.

Seeing a tax liability account on the income statement will cause a lender to pause and question the information. Now, it could be that the account is truly a tax liability account, OR it is possible that the account could be misnamed or mislabeled.

In the construction company example, there were quite a few accounts like this that had been miscategorized. The fix was simple – a good accountant can go into the chart of accounts and reclassify the account so that it shows up on the appropriate financial statement. In one case, the account was on the right financial statement, so the name was changed not to confuse a lender.

Third, are there accounts that have negative balances? This concept gets a little tricky. Any time we talk about negative and positive balances in accounting, we must understand what this means by definition. Here again, is the math problem people often think is the issue in accounting.

If you look at an income statement in QuickBooks, it would not be obvious to you that REVENUE accounts have credit balances (or what those in math circles would equate to as "negative" balances)....because they look like a positive number on the financial statement. However, when a revenue account is defined, the underlying balance should be a credit or negative number; however, the number will look POSITIVE when you look at the income statement. Confused yet?

I bet you are. Thus, if you looked at an income statement in QuickBooks and the revenue section looked like this:

```
Sample Income Statement
Revenue                $ 100,000.00
```

Figure 51   Sample - Correct Balance

Figure 51 shows exactly how revenue would be represented, even though behind the scenes, this represents a credit balance. However, take a look at this example:

In Figure 52, the minus sign is your indication that there is a problem here. This analysis works the same way with expense accounts or asset accounts, or liability accounts. Any minus sign could potentially be an issue.

```
Sample Income Statement
Revenue                -$100,000.00
```

Figure 52   Sample - Incorrect Balance

In the construction company case, they had several accounts that had minus signs in front of the balances. In some cases, it was because the accounts were not defined correctly, but some of it signified other major issues.

A large issue was the fact that wages were being reported and recorded incorrectly. That issue took some time to unravel, and that is where an accounting professional can help you make sure everything is corrected and works going forward.

Fourth, any accounts that appear personal. In the section on "Business versus Personal," you learned that personal and business accounts must be separated. Thus, you can have a business credit card, and you can have a personal credit card, but you should not have a credit card that serves both areas of your life.

Thus, several accounts had been identified as personal in the naming convention on the construction company's financial statements.

Upon questioning, it was confirmed they were personal. Thus, those balances needed to be written off.

Does this mean you can never use a personal card? No.... it just means that regularly, you show excellent business judgment and place business expense on a business credit card only. A mistake can happen....and suppose it does, on your personal credit card. In that case, you can have the pay from account be your business checking account. It is highly recommended that you make one payment for the one charge so that when it comes through your bank account as a payment, you can appropriately assign the correct vendor to the transaction and post the purchase documentation.

Finally, do your ratio analysis. As you learned in ratio analysis, this can tell you if you are overweight in liabilities and other issues. Run your ratio analysis as much as you can before going to a lender. You want to be prepared for the numbers they may examine, and that can give you a great idea of your financial position and any potential risks the lender may be concerned about in how the business works.

Part Six: Exercises, Practice, and Resources Learning activities:

1. As an entrepreneur, or if you want to be an entrepreneur, check out the Small Business Administration site. Find out what resources they have available and take one of their courses!

2. As an entrepreneur, or budding entrepreneur, start reaching out to SCORE in the Small Business Administration. Those executives could help you for many reasons – they can help you with marketing, product and service development, finance, and many other topics!

3. As an employee, make sure you are clear on reporting in the business. Are you educated on the purpose of different reports? Of course, today, this can be digital reports, not just paper reports, so educate yourself on the reporting that is crucial to what you do.

4. If you are acquiring a business, does the business have years of financial reports for you to review for trends? Make sure they have an income statement and balance sheet, and the cash flow statement can be important if you are assessing a business that has timing delays in the generation of cash flow. Also, look for aging reports on payables and receivables and as much data detail on product profitability and other important business measures. This is where SCORE executives can assist.

5. For your own business, make sure that reporting and data are being tracked for your business. Have access, easily, to financial reports and other financial and performance data on your business and ensure you have someone who can build that reporting for you.

6. Does the business have backup documents for transactions? This may not be 100% documented, but it is important to check. This documentation can be emails, it can be invoices, and other documents.

7. Interview a small business accountant if you are on the entrepreneur path. Find out what the accountant can do for you using this book as your basis for developing your questions.

8. Interview different accountants in the business you work for as an employee. Find out what they do and specifically, ask them how their role helps your department or ask them to give you ideas on what to watch out for around internal controls or problem solving on issues that come up around the financial data they care about from your department.

9. As an entrepreneur, work with your QuickBooks accountant, or other software, to find out how you can track more detail in your profit and loss/income statement. How might you utilize project tracking, or classes, in your reporting to identify product, service, or client profitability?

10. As an employee, ask a cost accountant or another accountant who may know your products or services' direct and indirect costs. What goes into these costs?

11. As an entrepreneur, find a SCORE executive or an accountant that can help you to determine the direct and indirect costs of your products and services. This activity could help you to revise pricing structures or help you find other opportunities.

12. As an entrepreneur, do you have a business plan? Even if the purpose is to vet out the idea in your mind, a business plan can be very useful. It becomes even more important if you need a funding source!

13. Have you separated your business expenses from your personal expenses? As you formalize a company, have a separate bank account and credit cards for your business.

14. As an entrepreneur, keep good records of transactions – including backup documentation (i.e., receipts).

15. If you are looking to buy a business, do they have good backup records of their transactions? Can you find receipts? Can you find invoices? Do they file things by paper copy or digitally?

16. If you are assessing a business to acquire, are the vendor and customer records up to date? Are 1099s current? Are tax payments current? Have bank reconciliations been completed? Are process and procedures done? Do they pay attention to internal controls? Are payroll taxes current?

17. As an entrepreneur, find a good accountant. You can find one through QuickBooks or ask around for a referral.

18. If you are acquiring a business, you may need the help of a CFO – someone who can help you assess the business. You can google for a CFO for hire, or a virtual CFO, and your accountant may know someone to refer.

19. Are you looking to sell your business? If so, a CFO and a wealth advisor can come in handy in helping you with the details of that transaction as well as how you will handle perhaps a large windfall of cash.

20. Interview an entrepreneur or two. Ask them about any of the questions and activities in this book. See what they have to say about the topics that interest you!

21. For a company you work for, many of these topics in this section can be great questions to ask about the company's accounting resources!

Notes

1 Internal control definition. Retrieved from https://www.accountingtools. com/articles/internal-control.html
2 Segregation of duties definition. Retrieved from https://www.accoun-tingtools.com/articles/segregation-of-duties.html
3 (2018). ABC Analysis & Cycle Counting in Inventory Control. Retrieved from https://gpmate.com/mate-pcs/abc-analysis-and-cycle-counting-in-inventory-control/
4 Martin, A. (n.d.). Implement Best Practices for Spreadsheet Use. Retrieved from http://www.s-ox.com/dsp_getFeaturesDetails.cfm?CID=2388
5 Microsoft (n. d.). Create a pivot table to analyze worksheet data. Retrieved from https://support.microsoft.com/en-us/office/create-a-pivottable-to-analyze-worksheet-data-a9a84538-bfe9-40a9-a8e9-f99134456576
6 Budget. Retrieved from https://www.investopedia.com/terms/b/budget.asp
7 Master budget (2020). What is it? Retrieved from https://www.thebal-ancesmb.com/budgeting-what-is-a-master-budget-393049
8 Cost driver definition. Retrieved from https://www.accountingtools.com/articles/2017/5/4/cost-driver
9 Variance analysis definition. Retrieved from https://www.accounting-tools.com/articles/what-is-variance-analysis.html
10 Flexible budget definition. Retrieved from https://www.accountingtools.com/articles/what-is-a-flexible-budget.html
11 Lang, B. (n.d.) How to use class tracking in QuickBooks. Retrieved from https://quickbooks.intuit.com/blog/whats-new/how-to-use-class-tracking-in-quickbooks/
12 (n.d.). Information Services Profit Margin 2007–2020. Retrieved from https://www.macrotrends.net/stocks/charts/III/information-services/profit-margins
13 Write your business plan. Retrieved from https://www.sba.gov/business-guide/plan-your-business/write-your-business-plan
14 Sole proprietorships. Retrieved from https://www.irs.gov/businesses/small-businesses-self-employed/sole-proprietorships
15 Limited liability corporation (LLC). Retrieved from https://www.irs.gov/businesses/small-businesses-self-employed/limited-liability-company-llc
16 S corporations. Retrieved from https://www.irs.gov/businesses/small-businesses-self-employed/s-corporations

17 IRS (n.d.). Topic no. 751 Social Security and Medicare Withholding Rates. Retrieved from https://www.irs.gov/taxtopics/tc751

18 Owners draw vs. salary: How to pay yourself (2020). Retrieved from https://bench.co/blog/accounting/owners-draw/

19 Self-employment tax (Social Security and Medicare taxes). Retrieved from https://www.irs.gov/businesses/small-businesses-self-employed/self-employment-tax-social-security-and-medicare-taxes

20 What does a CPA do? Retrieved from https://www.picpa.org/consumers/cpa-locator/what-does-a-cpa-do

21 What does a CFO do? Retrieved from https://corporatefinanceinstitute.com/resources/careers/jobs/what-does-a-cfo-do/

22 IRS (n.d.). Instructions for Forms 1099-MISC and 1099-NEC (2020). Retrieved from https://www.irs.gov/instructions/i1099msc

Appendices

Appendix A – Ratio Analysis Recap
Gross Profit Margin

$$(\text{Revenue} - \text{Cost of Goods Sold}) / \text{Revenue}$$

Year	Gross Profit Margin: Zoom			
YR1 2020	$ 507,262	/	$ 622,658 =	81.5%
YR2 2019	$ 269,516	/	$ 330,517 =	81.5%

Year	Gross Profit Margin: LogMeIn			
YR1 2019	$ 936,720	/	$ 1,260,385 =	74.3%
YR2 2018	$ 922,511	/	$ 1,203,992 =	76.6%

Net Profit Margin

$$\text{Net Income} / \text{Revenue}$$

Company	Zoom	
Year	Revenue	Net Profit
YR1 2020	$ 622,658	$ 26,362
YR2 2019	$ 330,517	$ 8,349
Company	LogMeIn	
Year	Revenue	Net Profit
YR1 2019	$ 1,260,385	$ (14,555)
YR2 2018	$ 1,203,992	$ 74,371

Solvency Ratios

Debt to Assets : Total Debt / Total Assets

Equity to Assets : Total Equity / Total Assets

Debt to Equity : Total Liabilities / Total Shareholder Equity

Year	Debt to Assets: Zoom			
YR1 2020	$ 455,902	/ $ 1,289,845	=	35.3%
YR2 2019	$ 202,452	/ $ 354,565	=	57.1%
Year	Equity to Assets: Zoom			
YR1 2020	$ 833,943	/ $ 1,289,845	=	64.7%
YR2 2019	$ 152,113	/ $ 354,565	=	42.9%
Year	Debt to Equity: Zoom			
YR1 2020	$ 455,902	/ $ 833,943	=	54.7%
YR2 2019	$ 202,452	/ $ 152,113	=	133.1%

Current Ratio : Current Assets / Current Liabilities

Quick Ratio : $($Current Liabilities – Inventory$)$ / Current Liabilities

Zoom			
2020	$1,095,522 / $333,830	=	3.28
2019	$ 276,719 / $152,341	=	1.82

LogMeIn			
2019	$ 327,893 / $524,666	=	0.62
2018	$ 324,951 / $622,657	=	0.52

Inventory Turnover Ratio : Cost of Goods Sold / Inventory

or

Cost of Goods Sold / $($ $($Inventory Current Period +Inventory Previous Period$)$ / 2$)$

Days Sales in Inventory : 365 days / Inventory Turnover Rate

Accounts Receivable Turnover : Revenue / Accounts Receivable

Revenue / ((accounts receivable current period
+ accounts receivable previous period) / 2)

Zoom

Revenue	/ Avg A/R	= A/R Turnover
$ 622,658	/ $ 92,024 =	6.77

LogMeIn

Revenue	/ Avg A/R	= A/R Turnover
$1,260,385	/ $101,475 =	12.42

Days Sales Outstanding : 365 days / Accounts Receivable Turnover

Zoom

Days in a year	/ A/R Turnover	= Days Sales Outstanding
365 /	6.77 =	53.94

LogMeIn

Days in a year	/ A/R Turnover	= Days Sales Outstanding
365 /	12.42 =	29.39

Accounts Payable Turnover : Total Purchases / Accounts Payable

(Cost of Goods Sold + Inventory Current Period − Inventory Previous Period)
/ ((Accounts Payable Current Period + Accounts Payable Previous Period) / 2)

Zoom

Cost of Goods Sold	/ Average A/P	= A/P Turnover
$ 115,396	/ $ 3,280 =	35.19

LogMeIn

Cost of Goods Sold	/ Average A/P	= A/P Turnover
$ 323,665	/ $ 43,776 =	7.39

Days Payable Outstanding

Zoom

Days in a year	/ A/P Turnover	= Days Payable Outstanding
365 /	35.19 =	10.37

LogMeIn

Days in a year / A/P Turnover = Days Payable Outstanding

365 /   7.39 =   49.37

Cash Conversion Cycle :

+ Days Sales Outstanding

+ Days Sales in Inventory

− Days Payables Outstanding

= Cash Conversion Cycle

Zoom	
Days Sales Outstanding	53.94
Days in Inventory	-
Days Payables Outstanding	(10.37)
Cash Conversion Cycle	43.57

LogMeIn	
Days Sales Outstanding	29.39
Days in Inventory	-
Days Payables Outstanding	(49.37)
Cash Conversion Cycle	(19.98)

Appendix B – Learning Plan

Use this information and Appendix F (Starting and Managing a Book Group) to learn the book's material.

Part One: Why Being Financially Savvy Matters
Part One should be of interest to investors, entrepreneurs, and employees. It is a chapter that
  builds the arguments for developing your financial competence.
Part One   Completed _____

Part Two: Revenue and Expense – The Basics of Income Statements

Part Two examines the foundational elements of the Income Statement. Entrepreneurs,
  employees, and investors will find value in reviewing this part of the book.
Profit and Cash   Completed _____
Revenue   Completed _____
Cost of Goods Sold   Completed _____
Gross Margin   Completed _____
Operating Expenses   Completed _____
Operating Income   Completed _____
Net Profit   Completed _____

Timing Issues	Completed _____
Part Two	Completed _____

Part Three: Assets, Liabilities and Equity – Understanding the Balance Sheet

Part Three is all about the balance sheet and exploring all of the parts and accounts of this financial statement. As an entrepreneur, investor, or employee, it is important to have a solid understanding of the information contained in this report.

Short Term vs Long Term	Completed _____
Cash	Completed _____
Accounts Receivable	Completed _____
Inventory	Completed _____
PP&E	Completed _____
Accounts Payable	Completed _____
Long-Term Liabilities	Completed _____
Stock/Retained Earnings	Completed _____
Part Three	Completed _____
Part Four: Cash Flow Statements	
Profit/Cash Relationship	Completed _____
Operating Activities	Completed _____
Investing Activities	Completed _____
Financing Activities	Completed _____
Fitting Them Together	Completed _____
Working Capital	Completed _____
Part Four	Completed _____

Part Five: The Power of Ratios

Ratios help you build upon the conceptual framework of the financial statements from the previous topics in the book. Now, you are utilizing your baseline understanding of financial statements and starting to interpret performance. This is a crucial learning exercise for employees, investors, and entrepreneurs.

Profitability Ratios	Completed _____
Gross Profit Margin	
Net Profit Margin	
Solvency Ratios	Completed _____
Liquidity Ratios	Completed _____
Current Ratio	
Quick Ratio	
Activity Ratios	Completed _____
Inventory Turnover	
A/R Turnover	
A/P Turnover	
Cash Conversion Cycle	
Other Ratios	Completed _____
EBITDA	
Free Cash Flow	
Horizontal Analysis	
Part Five	Completed _____

Part Six: Special Topics

This section of the book contains various topics that touch your lives as an employee or an entrepreneur. As an investor, you may not touch on these much at all – however, internal controls are always a concern, even as an investor, and you will expect businesses to keep control over their financial assets.

Internal Controls	Completed _____
Excel Controls	Completed _____
Budgeting	Completed _____
Variance Analysis	Completed _____
Contractors' vs Employees	Completed _____
Small Business	Completed _____
Part Six	Completed _____

Appendix C – Nomenclature Table

Throughout the book, certain terms have other terms by which they are known. This table is intended to be a quick reference as you are studying the presented material and analysis strategies.

WORD OR PHRASE	OTHER NAMES
Profit and loss statement	Income statement
	Statement of operations
	Consolidated profit and loss
	Consolidated income statement
	Consolidated statement of operations
Balance sheet	Consolidated balance sheet
Cash flow statement	Consolidated statement of cash flow(s)
Revenue	Sales
	Net sales
Accounts receivable	Accounts receivable, net
Cost of goods sold	COGS
	Cost of revenue
	Cost of sales
Net profit	Net income

In addition, sometimes, you may look up a ratio on Google or other web inquiry tool like Bing or Chrome. I have had many students look up a ratio for a company to check their work, and the number is a little bit different. Presented throughout the book are formulas for common ratios, but you may find a slightly different variation online. So how do you assess that?

For one, the difference in the calculation may be the author's preference about how THAT PERSON likes to calculate the formula. The reasoning could be valid, so be on the lookout as to WHY the person calculates it in a slightly different way.

Another reason may be that if you work FOR a company, you may have access to more precise data. Rather than the data, we may have an investor or an entrepreneur, which is especially true when calculating the accounts payable turnover. Internal calculations of this number are much more accurate because you can get your hands on more precise accounts payable data on purchases.

Finally, the ratio formula may be another interpretation of the information contained in the formula. For example, let us examine variations of the gross profit ratio.

You are learning that the formula is **Gross Margin/Revenue**. You could also see this as **Gross Margin/Sales**. Or you could see it represented as **Revenue – Cost of Goods Sold/Revenue**. But now, you KNOW that "revenue minus cost of goods sold" is equivalent to how "gross margin" is calculated, and thus you can conclude it is the same formula just presented in a different way.

Appendix D – Personal and Corporate Finance

PERSONAL Finance	CORPORATE FINANCE
We have discretionary income	A company generates a net income or estimated net income
We are building net worth	A company is building equity
We have an emergency fund	A company has free cash flow
We have INCOME	A company generates sales or revenue
We have expenses	A company has expenses
Households generally do not have costs of good sold	a company does have costs of goods sold or costs of revenues
We have assets	A company has assets
We have liabilities	A company has liabilities
We have cash flow	A company has cash flow
We are on a cash basis of accounting	Companies, if publicly traded, use accrual accounting. Otherwise, companies use the cash basis of accounting

Appendix E – Utilizing a Book Group

One of the best ways to handle learning this material is to have a few people study. Suppose you are an employee of a company. In that case, this can easily be accomplished by having your department learn together, or you have like-minded colleagues that want to leverage their knowledge of financial information for business and promotional opportunities.

As an investor, you may not be able to get your entire department interested in the information, but you may have friends or colleagues that have similar interests in building your financial intelligence.

As a budding entrepreneur, you may have friends or family that are interested in learning how to understand financial information about possible business investments. Plus, there are meet-up groups that could be interested in learning this material together, or you could start your own virtual meet-up!

Regardless of the reason you want to learn this material, here are various components of a learning group that you want to consider:

Facilitation

As you are learning the material, you may want to consider having accountants join in the conversation – for their expertise and the fact that they can help translate information if anyone struggles with the conceptual framework. It may be easy to find someone who works in a company that does a good job explaining information about the accounting world in a company.

Not everyone has access to individuals who can explain accounting information well. You can always look up SCORE executive through the Small Business Administration, especially if you are desiring to start a business. However, be aware that they may not be willing to be educators.

One other option is that you can utilize my expertise. Contact me at Info@coeurbridge.com to discuss what you would like to do, and we can set up the structure!

Company Selections

One thing to do is decide on at least a couple of companies that your group wants to study. If you are employees of a particular company, then you can choose the company you work for PLUS a competitor. The competitor should be a company where you can access their financial information, or it is a company that is publicly-traded that is similar to your company. Since you have a lot of intimate knowledge about your company, as you learn about different concepts in the financial world, you will have a much easier time connecting the information to your experience.

As an investor, you can choose any industry you are interested in and the companies within that industry. One good way to think about this is you may want to consider companies that you frequent as a customer. For instance, here where I live, I am a customer of Costco, Amazon, Starbucks, Microsoft, Alaska Airlines, and T-Mobile. Plus, I have worked for Weyerhaeuser, Starbucks, Boeing, and other areas. All of them would be great candidates to study for investments.

As a budding entrepreneur, you would want to study a company similar to the one that you want to start or purchase. Now, one thing to note, in terms of technology companies, some of the big companies out there like Google, Facebook, Microsoft, or Amazon are very complex with lots of divisions, departments, products, and services. Thus, building a small business is not an exact 100% comparison, but you can learn a lot by studying the larger companies and their financial statements and financial information. The entire purpose of studying these companies is to start understanding financial information with a company that INTERESTS you because you will give up learning the material with that interest.

Organizing the Sessions

As you can see, there is a lot of material to cover in this book. So, you have to have some strategies to think about in conducting sessions. Here are some ideas to get you started!

Option 1 – One option is to follow the questions and exercises in each section. Each section could take one to three sessions if you have an hour each session. Facilitating a study group in this applied manner may take several sessions until you get used to the material.

Option 2 – Another option is to follow a ten week schedule like a course I teach to graduate students.

Index

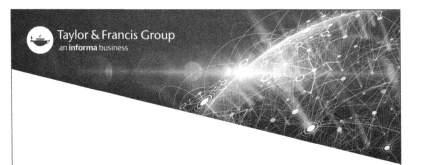

Printed in the United States
by Baker & Taylor Publisher Services